RESTORED

From Mourning to Dancing

Kerry-Ann Zamore Frazier

2

RESTORED

From Mourning to Dancing

Kerry-Ann Zamore Frazier

BASAR PUBLISHING

All Scriptures are taken from the New International King James Version

ISBN 978-1-942013-46-4

This book was printed in the United States

Photographer
Hatice Lance of LasPhotodeLance
(254) 702-6672. http://lasphotodelance.com/

Makeup Artist
Arrica Price (Madame Mua)
600 Indian Trail Dr.
Suite 108
Harker Heights, TX, 76548
254-319-0190

Edited by Crystal Daniels (Crystal Clear Brilliance)

Cover Design KDV Design & Associates, LLC

Dedication and Acknowledgement

I am grateful to the One who created and sustained me; the same One who has restored me to the joy of my salvation, my Lord and Savior, Jesus Christ. I thank God for his tender mercies and his grace; for knowing exactly what is best for me and for guiding me even when I didn't know it was He who was keeping me. Jeremiah 29:11 is my verse of solace. I repeated this verse on a daily basis during the lowest points in my life and I continue to do so even today. It reads *"For I know the thoughts I think towards you, says the Lord, thoughts of peace and not of evil, to give you a future and a hope."* I thank God for creating me, for my obstacles, all my hurts and for His perfect plan for me. He has truly shown me that His thoughts towards me are for my good. He has turned my mourning into dancing.

Also, I was fortunate to be born into a family who loves – The Zamore family from the Commonwealth of Dominica, in the West Indies. My family holds a special place in my heart because they truly have shown me the meaning of family. Thank you to my uncles for showing me what true men stand for and what the meaning of family looks like. Thank you to my aunties both biological and spiritual who have shown me the true essence of being a woman of God. A special thank you to auntie Bevo, my other mother. I love you to the moon and back.

This book is also dedicated to my family: my husband, Daryl, my sons Vincent and Andrew, my daughter Kayla and newest addition to the family, Landon. I wish to express deep appreciation to my darling husband, Daryl, for all your support and love; we are so much better together. To my awesome children, thank you for letting mommy write. Remember in everything you do, seek God, put Him first and everything falls into place. To sons, Vincent and Andrew in particular, we have been through a lot together, but you are witnesses that God is good and He is a keeper of His word. You have experienced a lot of hurt and pain, but you have also seen that God can use what the devil meant for evil and turn it into a blessing. Know that there is no weapon that is formed against you that will prosper. Thank you for your love and support. You are not your past; God has an awesome plan for both of you. Trust Him.

Lovingly, but surely not least, to my parents Denis and Kiran Greenidge, thank you for our talks, our laughs, and the admonition you gave me over the years. Thank you for being overprotective sometimes; thank you for challenging me and telling me no when I wanted to hear yes. This helped me to negotiate life in difficult times. Thank you for never giving up on me; thank you for making me work hard and for pushing me to be the best I could ever be. And most importantly, thank you for introducing me to Jesus; He is the best thing that ever happened to me.

To my cousin Ann, you have been a sister to me and I love you dearly. Thank you for always having my back and being my role model. To my "bestie" Nakia Shy. Thank you for being the true face of friendship. You've seen me at my worst and at my best and you have been my "Jonathan"; I thank you for your love and support. Thank you too, Samantha, my dear sweet friend and sister. You have been a wonderful support through divorce and the rebuilding.

Finally, I dedicate this book to all the women who remain silent victims of family violence. That is not God's plan for you. You can be free, you can live. Let Him restore you. God has so much more in store for you. Don't remain in bondage; it's hard and it's scary, but take the first step. Take your voice back. Call your local domestic violence shelter to begin again. You can live free from hurt, take your voice back.

FOREWORD

By

M. Ann Shillingford-Butler, Ph.D.
Associate Professor of Counseling and Education
College of William & Mary

Why did she stay with him? What was she thinking keeping her children in those violent conditions? These are questions that are often asked when society learns of situations of domestic violence. Author Kerry-Ann Frazier lays a very vivid picture of what it's like to endure spousal abuse. She goes into clear details in painting a picture of what it is like to remain in an abusive relationship, what the thought process is like during and after an abusive episode and what kept her going.

Domestic violence is a pervasive issue that continues to affect households around the globe. Domestic violence does not discriminate against race, age, or gender. However, statistics on domestic violence, particularly spousal abuse, is most prevalent against women. In fact, a significant percentage of women murdered involved a family member.

Although several authors have written on domestic violence and spousal abuse, this problem continues to corrupt relationships across society. Women should know and understand the signs of domestic violence not only based on their partner's violent behaviors but also from their own inner thought. What is your mind telling you about this relationship? Do you feel fear, numbness, or a sense of helplessness? Reflect on what this means for you and about your current relationship.

The signs are always there and what Kerry-Ann does with this book is take the reader into the very heart of women, who for years endured spousal abuse. She explores her own inner turmoil and her determination to survive. She explains how she embraced life for her and her children and her determination to fight this monster, spousal abuse. Kerry-Ann concludes the book by highlighting that through faith and the support of family she came out victorious...and alive.

FOREWORD

By

Anne Jackson JD Assistant District Attorney

Family Violence has fascinated me for years. I am not a survivor of it – I am one of the fortunate ones who knew and experienced none of it in my childhood. As an adult – as a professional - the idea that the very people who purport to love and trust us would physically harm us is preposterous. Yet, I see it every day as a lawyer.

The phrases one hears when one works in the family violence field frequently focus on the victim: "Wrap her in services" and "The victim is an expert on her own safety." As a prosecutor, I am interested in stopping the violence through holding the perpetrator accountable. Meeting the victim's needs and keeping the victim safe are a huge part of that process. Prosecutors and police officers want to keep victims safe, but we also REALLY want to put the bad guys away.

I quickly realized as a young prosecutor that I am not able to solve anyone's family violence problems on my own – with a successful prosecution or otherwise. What I realized sitting in my office day after day was that there is no way that a victim of violence in the home is going to testify or tell the truth when his/her basic needs are not being met. Why in the world would someone tell the truth about the most private, intimate and potentially humiliating events of her/his life, if doing so changed the very fabric of their lives? If doing so turned her husband into a criminal? In those early moments, I realized that the only way to affect family violence is by attacking it holistically – with a multi-disciplinary community-coordinated response.

A family violence assault is a crime against the "peace and dignity of the state." Family violence cases should be prosecuted as crimes, yet we cannot escape the fact that doing so affects kids and husbands and wives -- the most basic unit of our society. As such, all we should ask of victims/survivors should be: take care of yourself and let us do the rest. Raise your kids. Do your job. Be the best spouse you can be. After all, the decision of whether to make arrest for family violence is that of a peace officer. The decision whether to prosecute a case is that of a prosecutor. The decision whether to indict is that of a grand jury. And the decision of whether there is "guilt" is that of a judge or jury. The only thing we should ask of our "victims" is honesty and availability; always speak the truth and be where I can find you. Otherwise, do what mothers and fathers, sisters and brothers should do, raise kids. Do your job and be a good citizen, the system should take care of the rest – of holding family violence perpetrators accountable.

But do we? As a community? A society? A criminal justice system? Do you actually hold accountable people who perpetrate violence behind closed doors? Do I? Do We? Or do we expect victims to do it? Do we expect victims to "just leave"? Do we expect victims to testify? Do we expect victims to always put her/his children first? To simply seek marriage counseling and be a better wife/husband? To hire an attorney and file for divorce? Do we expect a victim to successfully navigate all of these things alone while the criminal justice system slowly finds a way to potentially prove a case beyond a reasonable doubt?

Or do we need a combination of all things - a system of social service responses that considers ALL of the needs of the family - the way Kerry-Ann Frazier has learned to do through years of personal and professional experience.

As you read this book, I hope you see the profound insight Kerry-Ann has gained about family violence as a survivor, mother, church member, social worker, advocate and friend of law enforcement. I hope you see that she has experienced how the church/faith-based institutions treat it. How the military has treated it. How different states treat it. How different government agencies, such as Child Protective Services, treat it. How non-profit organizations can be utilized by ALL of us. And keep in mind, that as she did so, she was dealing with family violence in her OWN home where she was raising HER boys. See if you can discern the calm reserve that she consistently exhibited, and the cunning, precise, well-articulated way that her perpetrator portrayed her part in it. And how it ALL came tumbling down and crystallized in a few tragic moments one fateful night when the police were called. And one additional day, when she heard her own voice on the 911 call in a lawyer's office.

I hope you clearly experience her story and her victory over it. And find within it a call to action of your own. Because quite frankly, we need your help.

FOREWORD

By

Minister Nakia O. Shy

I remember the first time Kerry came to my home. I remember getting a call in the middle of the night letting me know she was on her way with her two boys. I thought to myself *'why would she bring her two young sons out in the dead of winter, in Alaska no less. What could have possibly been so bad?'*

When she arrived I took the boys upstairs but first noticing that they were in their pajamas. Again I questioned *'Why?'* internally but kept those thoughts to myself and showed them where they would sleep. I came back downstairs and tried to engage Kerry in small conversation. She seemed so withdrawn but in the midst of just listening she let her dark secret out. It was that moment that I realized that my leader, mentor, and soon-to-be best friend was in a situation the church was not willing to face and was ill-equipped to deal with.

This book is a story of a woman who has endured the most tragic, demeaning, and possibly the most demoralizing ordeal. This is not a sob story or a cry for attention but the battle cry of victory. Kerry becomes bare in the pages following to give hope to the hopeless and to show that although battered you are not broken. That although you had bad things happen in your life, it is not the ending to your story, you can begin again, you can be Restored!

Preface

Sometimes when bad things happen to us, we are quick to say "Why God?" "Why me?" I have asked those questions often. I was angry at God for allowing bad things to happen to me and I was angry at my family for not seeing those things that happened to me. I was angry at myself for being a victim and I was angry at the world for not being hurt because I was hurting. I kept all my anger hidden deep inside and wore happy smiling masks most of my life. Every day I tried to be as pleasant as I could muster. I refused to let anyone know I was hurting, but inside I was dying. I had the most negative view of myself internally. Although I said all the right things and positive affirmations daily, I did not believe them. I had become a professional at pretending I was ok.

I was a church baby - I grew up in the church from an early age - so I knew all the right Scriptures to quote. When I became a social worker I knew all the therapeutic interventions and theories in practice, but I did not adhere to any of them. I was stuck in a cycle of internal self-hate and external false happiness.

When I finally admitted and accepted that I had been a victim and that it had not killed me, that although I was handed a bunch of lemons, I could chose to make lemonade. It was then and only then that I was able to move past all the hurt. Admittance was the first step to my healing.

Although I had been a church baby, I did not lean on my relationship with God because of the many false messages the church elders had given me regarding my abuse. I was thoroughly confused. I had to relearn who God was and then I repented to God and I forgave myself in order to move on. I had to verbally say to myself, "Kerry you were a child and someone took advantage of you. Kerry you wanted a happy family and you did your best. Kerry, God is not the author of your pain." I had been in a state of constant mourning. I mourned my lost innocence, I mourned the idea of a family that I did not have in reality. I mourned me, because I had completely lost myself in the cycle of domestic abuse. I had to make a decision to open my heart and mind to allow God to restore me and I finally found my smile and the joy of my salvation, my mourning had been turned into dancing.

Domestic abuse is not the period to your story, it is simply a semicolon before the real story begins.

This book is not just my story, it is the personal experience of over a million women in America. It is the personal experience of millions of women worldwide. It is the personal experience of women who live in silence and fear. This book is also the practical application of how I got through it and moved on. It is also a living witness that you can have the toughest start to life but still prevail when you put things into perspective.

Domestic abuse says you have no voice, this book says, "Take it back!"

Chapter 1

AWAKENING

I felt a heavy thud against my face, and then hot tears stung my eyelids as I winced in pain. I looked into his eyes and I saw it, this man hated me - there was no love, no caring, no compassion, and no resemblance of the man I called my husband for thirteen years. Rather, his face contorted into that of a raging beast, eyes red as a seething volcano, nostrils flared in anger, teeth gritting in disgust, fist balled for combat. His chest heaved heavily; I felt his hot breath against my neck. "You bitch!! I hate you, get out of my house or I'll drag you out!!" Before I could react, I felt the stinging pain of my hair being pulled from its roots as he proceeded to drag me across the floor. *How did I get here? Why didn't I see this coming? And why didn't I fight back? God, is he going to kill me? What will happen to my children if I die, and what will my parents say? I can't die like this. I refuse to die like this!* I began to fight with every muscle in my body; for every dirty word I took in, I fought. For every slap, shove and punch I had taken, I fought. For years of secrets, I fought. I fought and cried, and cried and fought. Who was this man? Damn it, who am I? God, you're gonna need to show up fast because I can't live like this anymore.

I had fallen in love with a beautiful, articulate, ambitious, educated monster. But he was my monster to protect against the wicked world who meant him harm. Besides, he was not bad all the time, so it's not really a big deal.

This was the lie I lived for thirteen years. Here I was 35 years old, well-educated with a double master's degree, two beautiful children, and a successful career, in social work no less, advocating for victims of abuse. I was a licensed minister, a playwright, a very friendly and appealingly outgoing woman who was the unhappiest she had ever been. Lord, get me out of this marriage! This man hates me and I hate him, I'm tired of faking, tired of praying and tired of counselors and counseling. Help me!

The God in me knew that this was the storm I had to go through; But the fear in me thought, *'How am I going to get through this?'* I had been awakened from years of denial with a solitary closed-fist punch to the temple. How did I get here? How did I allow this man to kill my spirit? Lord, I am not sure how, but I need You to help me come out of this alive and I promise I will be who You called me to be.

This journey began thirteen years prior in my college dormitory where I met, what I thought, was the most amazing young man. He was physically appealing to me. It's funny how the devil knows exactly how to appeal to our eyes. He was tall, light-skinned with curly black hair and light eyes, and had an incredibly athletic build; just my type. He was well-dressed and very well-spoken, unlike a lot of the college students on my campus. I was heartbroken over a former relationship with my first love. It was a relationship that ended prematurely without closure. I was hurt and vulnerable and needed a friend. Mr. Tall, Light-skinned and Good-looking was that friend. We talked and laughed and developed a close relationship very quickly. I was head over heels in love and he had sworn his love for me stating that he never wanted me out of his sight because of how much he loved me. I thought he was the sun and the moon; he loved me more than any person ever had. However, as the Holy Spirit always does, he began to show me signs that this relationship may be dangerous. I often performed in community plays as well as fashion shows as a hobby and after one particular show, my boyfriend, Mr. Tall, Light-skinned, and Good-looking, showed me a side of him that caused my blood to run cold. I was excited from the success of the show and enthusiastically chattered with several male and female friends afterward. Unknowingly, Mr. Good-looking was growing more and more irate at the fact that I had been communicating with my male friends.

We left the community center and I continued my happy chattering about the fashion show as he drove in complete silence. I thought he was listening to my excitement. We drove along the Potomac River at approximately fifty miles per hour when he suddenly slammed on the brakes. The car came to a screeching halt as it spun into a parked position. "Don't you ever embarrass me like that again!" he shouted. I blinked terrified not understanding what was going on. "Do you understand how much I love you?" I was horrified! His angry words and cold stare cut through the silence in the car. He was in a parked position barely off the highway. I was fearful that a car could come at any moment and slam into the parked car that was barely off the road. I wasn't sure what to say or what to do, so I apologized.

I had never had such an encounter with anyone before. I felt that I had somehow hurt him or embarrassed him by being friendly with other men. I was afraid, shocked and unsure of what to do. I knew in my heart that his behavior was extreme and rather absurd, but with my limited experience dating I also considered that maybe I was wrong, maybe he loves me so much he was trying to protect me from something I was otherwise unaware. But what if

I'm wrong? What if this man is scary and harmful to me? I looked into his face searching for some hope that he truly loved me. He buried his hands in his face and began to sob, his eyes welling with tears. "Don't you see how much I love you?" he whispered, a hoarse, teary whisper. "I can't lose you baby, I'm sorry. I just can't lose you."

Although his behavior was very odd to me, I wanted to care for him, I wanted to comfort him, I wanted to believe that his love ran so deep and so strong that he couldn't bear the thought of me with anyone else so he overreacted. I wanted to believe that this was an isolated incident. My tears matched his and I buried my face in his neck. "Your friends are causing issues with us baby, I don't want to share you," he said. "I just need you to leave these friends behind and focus on us."

I thought he was right. The only time we fought, involved a third party. He was never really upset with me, but rather someone else who he thought interfered with our relationship. Before long, I had begun to distance myself from not only my roommates, and social circles, but also my cousins, other family members and church members and anyone who took time away from him. I also quit community theatre as well as my modeling club. I quit any group that took time from him. I turned down an internship that would take time away from us and I even moved my dorm room to his floor to ensure he knew that I was close to him. But it never seemed like it was enough. He was weary of college and wanted to join the military. I didn't want to lose him.

Six months later I was standing at the altar waiting for my life to begin as his wife. I was completely isolated from anyone who knew me and, most importantly, those who cared for me. I was completely alone. My friends were shocked at the announcement of our nuptials and even more that I had also decided not to return to campus. They questioned why I would leave college to enter into a marriage with someone they believed I barely knew. I was defensive and I defended my actions, but I, too, had reservations. I wasn't sure why, but the relationship didn't feel right to me, but, I made a commitment, I had promised him I would be there and I needed to keep my promise.

My hands shook, holding my bridal bouquet. *Please don't prolong this any further. I need to get to the altar. I need to get this dreaded day over with. Why had he called me hours before the wedding? And what was he so angry about? A shirt? What shirt was he talking about?* My mind raced desperately trying to figure out what he was upset about.

About two hours before the wedding my tall and light-skinned fiancé had called yelling angrily through the phone that he thought I had cheated on him. I was annoyed. I tried to contain my annoyance by smiling as my bridesmaids looked on questioningly. I couldn't let them know we were fighting. I needed to let everyone know I was making the right decision; I refused to look scared or unhappy. I needed to maintain my composure. I didn't need one more question from anyone about why I was getting married. After six months of dating, the accusations had become second nature. If a man looked, smiled or God forbid tried to have a conversation with me, I was accused of flirtation or an impending affair. I had to make certain that I stayed clear of all males.

I listened to his ranting and yelling on the phone. He was yelling about a football jersey he found in a box in our new apartment. I had no idea what jersey he was referring to. "Lord, I don't want to get married!" I thought and then quickly dismissed it. He scares me, but here I was, standing outside the door waiting to walk down the aisle. *'Lord, if this door remains closed for one second longer I may run out of this building,"* I thought in a panic. I recall looking at my dad hoping he would say something, but he didn't, he smiled at me and I couldn't stand to tell him I was unhappy and I was too good at pretending I was ok. No one knew that I wasn't.

Suddenly the sanctuary door opened and there he was standing at the altar, looking amazingly handsome and cold. His stiff smile did not meet his eyes, they were stoic. I had begun to recognize his expressions and the smile was second nature. He was displeased with something. I swallowed sadly. I looked at the guests and smiled, as I slowly made my way down the aisle. Why am I doing this? Lord, I don't really want to do this. My hands shook, I can't disappoint my family. Everyone is here for this wedding. How do I stop the wedding? Everything is paid for; everyone is here, God please! I can't back out. Fine! I'll just do it; maybe things will be better when we are married. Maybe he won't be so insecure anymore. Maybe the arguments will stop. After all, we will be married, so why would he accuse me of cheating.

Twenty minutes later, I was married. Thirteen years later, I stared into the eyes of a police officer. "Ma'am, has this happened before?" I blinked, wondering how long he had been talking to me. He repeated the question, "Has this happened before?" I looked up at him, my mind racing frantically, has this happened before? I stared at him in silence, but my mind was screaming, *'You mean has he hit me? Dragged me across the floor? Yes!* My mind screamed, *'Yes! Yes, he has dragged me, slapped me, and punched me! Yes he has! Yes he has humiliated me in front of friends, in front of my children. Yes, yes he has!'* But instead I looked away, I didn't want to talk. I didn't want these strangers judging him. I didn't want these strangers taking away everything we built. I didn't want them asking me any more questions. And what about my boys? My sweet boys had barricaded themselves in their rooms placing the desk on top of the dresser behind the door. My boys, didn't deserve this. What would happen to my children if I talked to them? What did the boys say to them? They actually saw him beating me this time. So many times before I was able to protect them from seeing their mommy hurt, but this time he didn't care. This time was different, this time he could have killed me.

How did this fight begin? Like so many others over the past thirteen years, I had said or done something that he felt was offensive to him. Whatever the argument, I was somehow at fault; I had caused the discord and he simply reacted to my action. That particular night I was once again accused of having an affair. I had arrived late from a church function and he sat in the dark waiting for me. Sitting in the dark waiting for me was not an unusual occurrence. He often sat in the dark smoldering when he was upset. It was meant to be intimidating, and it was. On one occasion he sat in the dark cleaning his gun at the table. I could hear the clicking sounds in the dark. It unnerved me, I was fearful, but never thought he would hurt me with a weapon.

When I opened the door, the house was silent as he sat on the couch waiting for me. There was an ominous tone in the house and I knew there was an impending fight so I was cautious. The children were already asleep in their beds. The house was eerily still. Then the questions began flying at me like a firestorm. "Where have you been? Who were you talking to?" The accusations of an affair came. He said he had placed spyware on my computer and had been tracking my movements. He knew there was no affair, because there was nothing in my communications with anyone which suggested an affair but he continued the firestorm of questions getting angrier and angrier; he was out of control. He considered communication with another man an affair, and I had communicated with other men I considered friends. When he confronted me, I tried to exit the room and each time he barred the doorway with his large frame preventing me from leaving the room. I was afraid, but I knew I had to remain calm not to escalate his anger.

After almost an hour of questions and accusations I was able to go upstairs to check on the children who were sleeping. I decided to sleep upstairs. I logged on to my computer and began to look through emails when I heard his angry footsteps. Then the violence came, He grabbed me with one hand while his fist landed on my temple with one harsh blow. My younger son was witness to the ferocity and screamed for him to stop, placing himself between us. Without regard for his young son, he angrily brushed him aside causing him to fall. *'This can't be happening,'* I thought. *'He has completely lost it.'* This time was different, he didn't care; there was intense hate as he broke my fifteen inch laptop across his lap, shattering it into pieces. I was now horrified at the intense anger and force it took to snap a laptop in half. This man physically snapped my laptop in half. I knew then that he would hurt me with no regard to my life.

I began to sob listening to my son's cries, "Stop daddy! Leave my mommy alone! Stop! Don't hurt her! Don't hurt my mommy! Stop daddy!"

He didn't care, "Your mom is nothing but a lying whore, and she's a bitch!" "Get out of my house!" he spewed heatedly, as he tried to drag me out the house. As he dragged me, I fought him and cried feeling absolutely devastated. I lay at the bottom of the stairs looking up at the balcony at my son, whose face was horrified, as tears streamed down his cheeks. *'I can't do this to my baby,'* I thought. *'Lord, help! Lord, why can't you fix this? Lord, how did I end up here? Lord fix this! fix this please!'* I prayed.

It was 3 a.m. and the police officers were still asking questions and looking through my home. This new home we had just purchased this beautiful house which now seemed so cold and devoid of life and love. I stared blankly at the family pictures on the wall. The family in the picture seemed so far from reality of what happened just a few hours before. This was all a lie. This life we lived was a horrible lie. "Ma'am, can you tell us what happened?" the officer repeated again, jolting me back to my dismal reality. I looked up at him. My head throbbed; I just wanted to be left alone. The officer's large frame loomed over me. I didn't know what to do; if I spoke to these people his career, my career, our life would all be in jeopardy. But then I wondered, *What if I didn't?* This beautiful monster, who had struck me several times, dragged me and degraded me in front of our children, what else could he possibly do to hurt me?

My head throbbed. I could feel the small knot which had begun to swell at my temple. I was tired. My jaw hurt. My lip had begun to swell and my shoulder, back, thigh and buttocks ached from being dragged. I wanted to shower, but they were still here, still asking questions. The female officer came to my side, "Ma'am, what happened?" I looked into her soft, kind eyes; her small frame eagerly waited for my answer. She seemed sincere, but I was not going to let my guard down. No, not again. I had trusted police officers before; they had the power to destroy me. They have the power to destroy us. *I'll tell them enough to leave me alone,'* I thought. But I would not trust another police officer.

Almost ten years earlier, on Mother's Day no less, I had trusted police officers. I was curling my hair as my three-month-old infant slept soundly in his car seat. His two-year-old brother sat quietly on the carpet next to the car seat coloring in his Barney story book. I had carefully pulled my shoulder length hair into a bun at my nape leaving a few tendrils loose. I felt pretty in my brand new baby blue dress my mother had sent me as a Mother's Day present. "Who is this dude?" my husband had said coldly from the doorway. Before I could answer he stepped into the small bathroom in one quick step. "Why is this man emailing you?" he asked again angrily. I paused in fear not knowing what to say. I didn't know what he was talking about. I hadn't seen an email. Almost a year earlier my husband had convinced me that we only needed one email account. Busy with two children I very rarely checked the account so I didn't care about sharing an account.

"What are you talking about?" I asked, in barely a whisper.

"Don't you ever disrespect me like that; some girl and some dude that you knew emailed you congratulating you on your new baby, that's disrespectful to me!" I blinked and quickly began to apologize as I had done so many times before, but this time he was too angry. When I asked to see the message he became unglued, slapping me and knocking me off balance. I felt my body hit the floor heavily and as I lay with my face to the wet tile. I saw my oldest son dragging the car seat with his baby brother to his room, his eyes wide in fear.

I couldn't move; the tears didn't fall. *'If I stay down, he will stop yelling,'* I thought. *'Don't fight, just agree and he will stop.'* But that day, it didn't work.

"I don't know what you're talking about," I yelled as he grabbed a handful of hair and dragged me to a standing position. I stood up and still somewhat hunched over I began to push him. He slapped me again then forced me into the wall preventing me from running away. After we had tussled for a few minutes, he left the home shouting vile, venomous profanities.

A few minutes later my neighbor, Ms. Jackie, who had heard the ordeal came over without ringing the doorbell. She let herself in, stating that she had heard everything and called the police. It was not the first time she had checked on me, but it was the first time she called the police. Jackie had seen me and my home in disarray from a night of combat before, but this time she seemed shaken. Still dressed in her pajama bottoms and a T-shirt, she retrieved ice from my refrigerator and ordered me to place it on my cheek.

Jackie had become very astute in recognizing my moods and my signals. She knew not to speak when she saw me in the yard with my husband. He would often smile and wave and she would respond politely, but I knew she was keeping an eye on him and an eye on the children and me. Jackie had been my neighbor for almost a year and she had heard many fights since she and her family had moved in, so I knew she would respond as soon as he left. The military police officer arrived within thirty minutes because Jackie called when she heard the fighting. I was nervous; I didn't want to talk to them, but Jackie had convinced me that I needed to talk to someone. I trusted them and their authority, so I told them what happened. Did I feel safe? Well, I had never thought about it before. I never questioned whether or not I was safe, I simply existed as we were.

That night I agreed to stay with a friend in a safe place so I packed my bags and my sweet children and we stayed with a friend for the night. I saw tears in Jackie's eyes as we left. I had been on the installation less than two years and I knew very few people, but she and I had become very neighborly. I didn't want friends. I didn't want anyone to know what went on in my home. I kept my distance as much as possible. Over the almost four years of marriage I had learned to keep my distance; I lived with the personal mantra not to let anyone close to me see the dysfunction of our relationship.

Lizzie was a nurse, a young captain who I had befriended during one of my prenatal appointments. I knew I would be safe in her home. I tried to sleep but couldn't. I needed to know what would happen next. I was afraid of what would happen upon my return home. I had nowhere else to go. I had no money, I had no support. I was stuck. I tossed and turned uncomfortably on the couch until I finally gave up the idea of sleep. I lay awake, watching my children sleep on the makeshift bed on the floor. They didn't deserve this. They needed more. I needed more.

The next morning Lizzie, one of my only friends, cooked breakfast quietly observing me. She finally broke her silence when I told her that I would be going back home when she went to work. Her back stiffened and she continued to cook with a clear change in her mannerism. I knew she was angry, and disappointed.

"How long has this been going on?" she asked pointedly without looking at me.

"I don't know. I don't know when the hitting started" I answered honestly. She scolded me on being better than that and reminded me of my responsibility to my children. She also reminded me that as a military officer and nurse, she had a duty to report. My heart sank. Lizzie kept on talking, but I didn't hear her. She was upset, she was disappointed. This was my deepest fear. She continued that she hoped he never made rank because his kind didn't need to be in leadership. She was furious, but I didn't understand why. I felt sick. What had I done? I needed a friend; I needed a friend to support me and help me through this horrible ordeal. I immediately regretted telling her anything. I began to think fast, I didn't want her calling his command so I explained that I had planned on going to counseling at the chapel and asked her to give me time to work it out in counseling. As a military family I knew that my actions had a direct impact on his career. I knew that any undesirable actions would count against him making the next rank so I was careful not to let anyone know about our home life. I knew the chaplain was confidential so I convinced her that I would seek help there. She helped me call a chaplain to set an appointment and agreed to wait on calling anyone within his chain of command. I vowed then that I would never share my feelings or my marriage woes with her again.

Later that day I was contacted by military police. The officer explained that my husband didn't know where I or his children were and he was deeply concerned. I also discovered that he was not arrested or detained. He was questioned and he denied any violence citing that we simply had an argument and I left with the children. The officer continued that my neighbor had given them the phone number to where I spent the night. The officer's admonition to me was that I needed to come home with the children because it would be viewed as kidnapping. How could I kidnap my own children? I told the police officer that my husband had struck me which resulted in me leaving. I explained to him that my neighbor called and reiterated the ordeal from the night prior. He listened quietly, and then told me that my husband was concerned about his children. He asked me if I would return to the home. I said, "Yes." I was alone with my children and there was no one to trust. My friend had lectured me and told me she would report it if I didn't get help, and the police officer dismissed my claim of abuse.

So, thirteen years later, here I was again, I looked into the eyes of a police officer who wanted to know what happened and I recalled the last time I asked for help. I didn't trust him, I didn't trust her; but, I needed someone to believe me. I needed someone to fight for me. I needed someone to help me. I needed to trust someone. I needed to take a chance. The officers looked into my face. The female officer very quietly said to me, "Ma'am, this is not going to get better, I can see that you and your husband have been arguing, I need you to tell me what happened."

The male officer went to my boys who had barricaded themselves in the room. I wanted

38

to tell her what happened, but I knew I couldn't tell all. I didn't know if I could trust her yet. I thought that if I told her everything, they would take my children; they could destroy him so I began to tell only what I wanted them to know. I dared not shed all our secrets. "He hit me, he dragged me," I said. My heart was racing. It was the truth, I told someone. I had not been able to say those words out loud to anyone before. I waited for her expression. It was blank. Her eyes didn't judge me. I felt tears sting my eyelids. I waited for her to say something, but she didn't; she just listened patiently. I didn't want to trust her, but I felt the load and stress lighten by sharing a little bit of our dysfunction. I knew I was being set free. I could not contain the tears, so I began to weep.

'Damn!' I thought, *'Stop crying! Stay strong, you cannot break down now!'* but the tears refused to stop flowing. I wept for all the years I couldn't weep. I wept for my children who had seen so much; the fights had become second nature to them. I wept for my monster I so desperately loved and hated. I wept for the promise of what should have been and I wept while shedding years of lies. I had not intended to speak up, but I couldn't contain my mouth. My pain had decided to speak up. I knew in my head that in speaking I was expressing that I refused to be a victim anymore. I refused to be broken. I refused to be any less than I was

created to be. I decided to tell the officer what transpired that night. I was afraid to write it. Writing the police report seemed so final, so real. I wrote the report hesitantly. But I prayed that these officers would truly help me.

I watched as they carried my husband away in handcuffs. "God please incline your ears to me, keep him safe tonight and get us through this." I prayed quietly.

When we decide to allow God to be in control, it is miraculous how things, no matter how bleak they appear, begin to work out for our good. After the police officer left early that morning, I was left alone with my children and the weight of the secrets I had shed. I had no one else to turn to. I was completely alone. I knew no one because we were still new to the state. My only supporters were thousands of miles away in other states. After my husband was arrested that night I sat in complete fear of the unknown. My boys slept restlessly in my bed as I sat up keeping watch over them. Every noise I heard that night scared me. I knew morning would come and with that the worst was yet to come. I knew he was angry, and humiliated, but I didn't know just how it would manifest itself.

Two weeks had passed since that awful night when my marriage came to a crashing halt and I had not heard from or seen my husband. So many things had transpired, I was numb, angry, sad, depressed, yet calm - this was my threshing floor.

Early Thursday morning after I dropped the boys off to school, I sat frozen at the drive-up teller machine unsure of what else to do. I looked at the screen again - it had not changed - balance $2.00. *'This has to be a mistake,'* I thought to myself. Then I thought of my husband. He had been released on bond and he was very angry. Would he? Could he? I could not believe that he would take all the money from the checking account.

One of our mutual friends had called me the day prior asking me if I needed anything. Of course I said, "No." The kids and I were fine. I still tried to keep up appearances, because I didn't want to let my friends know the level of our dysfunction. Our friend cautioned me that he had spoken with my husband who sounded very bitter. He indicated that during the course of the conversation my husband stated that he would leave me penniless; that his mission was now to destroy me as he felt I had destroyed him. I dismissed what our friend told me citing that is was just talk. There is no way he would leave his boys without. *'He may hate me, but he knew I had to take care of the children,'* I thought.

I went into the bank and stood in line. *'Lord, you know I'm not working, please tell me that he didn't take all the money from the account.'* As soon as the thought entered my mind I bit the tears back refusing to let them flow. I began to pray silently, "Lord, you know I left my thriving career to move here with him and I am not working. If he has taken all the money what am I supposed to do?"

The teller called out to me, "Ma'am!" *'How long had she been calling me?'* I thought looking around embarrassed. I gave her my account number and asked for a balance. She looked back at me blankly, and then slid a receipt to me. I read the receipt: checking $2.00, savings $0.00. Yes, he had done it. He had taken all the money from the accounts. The tears spilled quickly down my cheeks and then onto the floor. The teller eyed me sorrowfully. I wanted to run out of the bank, but instead, with all the dignity I could muster, I asked for a manager. The older lady came quickly to my side after the teller dialed her number. She led me to her office and I sat numbly. "Ma'am there was at least $5,000 in my checking account two days ago, and about $10,000 in my savings, I'm confused why there isn't any money in there now," I said between tears explaining the zero balance in my account.

She looked through my account history and quietly looked at me. "Ma'am is there anyone else on the account" she asked. I told her my husband and gave his name. "Your husband withdrew the money." I explained our current separation and asked if he could legally take all the money. The older lady looked at me sympathetically. "Yes, he can take all the money. This is Texas. Community property means the money belonged to both of you, and yes, he can take all or half just as you could have done the same." WHAT? My mind was reeling. The tears flowed, she handed me a tissue. "You might need an attorney, Kerry," she said to me in a quiet voice.

My husband had transferred all the money a few days prior, the account was correct, there was nothing there. I left immediately, my mind racing. Why? Why would he do that? After years of working together to save and to build; "Lord, what lesson is this?" I asked out loud. I calmly called the number that was so familiar and yet seemed so unfamiliar to me. I needed an explanation. I needed to know why he would do this. His voice came across the line. "My attorney advised me not to speak with you," and he hung up.

Tears stung my eyes again. Is he serious? Is this real? Lord, where are you and what am I supposed to do? What am I learning from this? I drove home my eyes filled with tears. I sat in the walk-in closet, which now bare of all his belongings, and wept. I called our mutual fund accounts and other savings and investment plans, and each one bore a current record of $0.00. He had taken everything we had. "Lord, help me." I began to hyperventilate, my heart raced, "How did I end up here?" I thought of the bills which were almost due, the mortgage, the electric bill, groceries, and my children. Lord, how? I curled up into a small ball in the back of the walk-in closet and cried. Was God punishing me? Was I mistaken in telling anyone about the abuse? Where was the help? Where were the advocates who said they would help me?

I was alone, I was broken and broke and I knew no one. I cried again until I fell asleep. A few hours later I heard the front door open as the alarm chimed. My sons were home from school and they needed mommy to be strong and calm. One more prayer - "Lord, please, I need you, I trust you, do it; whatever it is you need to do, do it and keep me through it." I had to place my trust completely in God. I had prayed for years for God to intervene on my behalf, I had even prayed for God to use whatever method He chooses to bring my husband to him even if it meant breaking us. I knew God was at work, because even in the worst I felt his presence and his love. I quickly washed my face as the boys came running into my room. I turned to them smiling, the familiar mask I had learned to wear so many years ago. I had to be happy mom - no sadness, no fear.

I looked into the eyes of my innocent boys. They looked around the house knowing their father's belongings had disappeared.

"Mommy, can we make brownies or a cake?" my younger son exclaimed.

"No, can we watch TV in your bed with you?" my older interjected.

"How about we do both," I responded, choking back my tears. The boys looked up at me searching my face trying to understand my emotions.

"Mommy, are you ok?"

I smiled. "No, not really, but I will be." "How about you kiddo, are you ok?" I asked both boys.

"We're fine mom," my younger son said melodiously answering for him and his brother.

"We just want you to be ok," my older stated looking at me quietly. He was always watching me, searching for any sign that I wasn't ok. I had to be strong for him in particular because I knew he was very angry with his father. He had seen and heard a lot but he internalized everything burying himself in books and academic success. I needed to be strong for him.

"Well how about we get started on a yummy treat," I smiled touching his cheek gently. "Lord, please keep my children; protect their hearts and minds from this mess and give me the words to say to them," I prayed silently. As I looked at my boys, I knew the journey ahead was going to be rough and hard, but I also believed that whatever it was, we would get through it.

I think the most frustrating experience at this point was everyone who I thought would be there to help me through the process was now gone. My advocate quickly walked me through the process handing me several resources and phone numbers to follow up on. In retrospect she did her best; but, I was unfamiliar with the area, unfamiliar with military protocol and I had no idea where to begin. The time that I needed from her to help me understand the process as well as help me come to terms with my failed, dysfunctional, abusive marriage could not be afforded to me because of the multiple cases she already had. This was the fear I had in revealing this secret to anyone. Often times I found in my life that people were well-intended but they very seldom followed through. I knew my advocate was well-intended, I just didn't feel supported. I felt that I was another case to get services to. She didn't know me, nor did she care who I was. She did her job, she connected me to the services she could, but I needed more. I needed to know the process. I needed to understand what would happen next.

Several years prior while we were still stationed in Germany we had an incident of family violence. This incident in Germany was almost two years after I had given birth to my younger son. My younger son was now almost three years old. My husband and I had become proficient in combat in the home. We fought, fist to fist, punch for punch, slap for slap. We made up, had a period of calm then went back to fighting again. It was a normalized dysfunction that had become second nature to me. I had also become proficient in masking my feelings. This particular incident of violence was very scary. It had been raining all day and the kids and I had been confined to the house. That evening, my husband and I argued, but I don't recall exactly why the discord had begun. I recall that he left the home in rain when I indicated that I was calling the police for help. I was at my wits' end and I needed help. The military police picked him up walking alongside the road in the small neighboring German village and placed him into custody. I was taken to the emergency room and treated for minor injuries. My neighbor, Jackie, had moved and after three years I had made new friends.

I called a couple I met through church. Two of my girlfriends as well as their husbands came to my home. As they entered the home they looked around taking everything in. I too began to looking around as I surveyed their startled expressions. The lamps and coffee table had been turned over. Several pictures were shattered. My husband had thrown family pictures against the wall breaking the glass, causing debris throughout the hallway and living room. My lip was busted and I was bruised in several areas. My girlfriends' expression said it all. They were fearful for me. Their husbands who outranked my husband were concerned about his career and they suggested that we call family advocacy to handle the matter internally. My husband had been awaiting news on a promotion, so they wanted to ensure his promotion would not be affected. The husbands explained that whatever we decide to do, we would need his career so I should help protect it and I agreed. My girlfriends drove me to the emergency room with my boys in tow. The nurses spoke with me quietly asking me about our relationship. They urged me to talk to an advocate and I did reluctantly. I was tired of talking to people. I was tired of the expression of pity in their eyes. I didn't want pity, I wanted help.

The advocate was aloof when she arrived. She seemed bothered as she went about documenting the details that I had given her. But I was ready to leave so her demeanor did not deter my decision. "Ma'am, I see you had a case two years ago," she mentioned irritably. I told her what transpired two years prior stating that it had been a hellish four years of marriage. I was ready to leave. We were not working and I was tired of fighting. I welcomed the escape. I told her we went to counseling with the chaplain for two sessions. She didn't pursue the topic further, but rather she asked what I had planned on doing this time. I told her I was leaving the marriage. She documented her notes and I never heard from her or saw her again.

I left that night with my children and went to stay with my parents who were stationed in the Netherlands. Soon after our move to Germany my parents themselves had accepted a tour of duty in Holland which was only three hours away from us. I was relieved and embarrassed but I was ready for the change. I thought it was my fresh start. I had contemplated how I would begin again. I had recently completed my bachelor's degree, and I was an experienced teacher and trainer. I thought I could work as a teacher. But where would I go? Because my parents had moved to Europe I had no place to return to in the States. I had been isolated from everyone for almost five years. When I realized that I had nowhere to go my joy was short-lived.

In the midst of contemplating how I would start my life over again, I learned of several mandatory appointments I needed to attend because of the investigation. The social worker at hospital as well as the military police had triggered another family advocacy investigation. I didn't want to return to the home, but I knew I needed to comply with the investigation. I recalled the police officer who told me leaving with the children could be considered kidnapping.

I didn't want any trouble. I didn't want to lose my children. I had also spoken to my husband who was devastated. He expressed that he didn't think he would live if I took his family away from him. He had threated suicide before and I had never taken him seriously, but this time he sounded so lost; I felt a deep sense of responsibility. I couldn't let him get hurt. I needed to go back, I needed to make sure he was ok and I needed to speak to the investigator. After almost two weeks away I had returned home cautiously hopeful for a change. I had decided not to give my parents the full details of what was going on in my life. They knew the marriage was in jeopardy, but they had no idea the full extent of what I was hiding and I was too ashamed and prideful to let them know.

Upon returning home, my husband was apologetic, he filled the home with laughter of little boys by playing with them every chance he got. He had become the father and husband I had dreamed of and my boys were happy and thrilled to have their dad. We took long family walks and vacationed together. We talked calmly about our problems and he had even begun to go to church with me. I was elated! The marriage I had prayed for was now a reality. I thought the bad times, the dysfunction and abuse was over. We went to our family advocacy counselor as well as counseling with our chaplain. We made friends and actually attended functions together as well as entertained friends in our home.

During our sessions we sat with the Family Advocacy therapist and I minimized our dysfunction painting the incident as an isolated fight. I needed to save him. I needed this happiness to last. He was so happy, so calm; I knew I needed to do everything I could to keep our happiness. He thanked me for the support and swore it would never happen again and although I had heard this many times before, this time I felt it was different because family advocacy was involved. The military was aware that we had problems so there would be no more fights. I felt safe. But it was ephemeral.

After a few months with our family advocacy social worker she informed us that our case was which was substantiated for family violence was being closed and that she wanted my husband to continue individual counseling. He was angry. He accused me of telling her something about him. He began to revert to his old self. He complained about the children's toys, the noise they made, my church friends calling or coming by, my involvement with church activities. He didn't want anyone to come over; he referred to them as "my noisy church friends". He argued that he felt I had betrayed him in calling the police. He blamed me for not making his rank and suggested that his career was over because of me. He even complained if

I touched him while we slept sometimes insisting that I sleep on the floor, which of course I refused to do. I felt like I lived in a house made of egg shells and I walked very carefully not to break them. I was stressed and he had become sullen and moody again. Once again, I was miserable and found myself wishing for an escape that never came. I thought of the therapy sessions and wished I had been honest with the therapist, but now the time had passed by. I was back in the cycle of our dysfunction with no escape. I dared not leave him, I had nowhere to go.

Now thirteen years later I found myself in the same predicament on another military installation. The advocate had given me several phone numbers of shelter services as well as counselors. She has also given me handouts on domestic violence. I didn't want to read any handouts she had given me and I definitely was not going to a shelter with my children. I looked around my beautiful home I had furnished with expensive collectable items. *'I can't go to a shelter,'* I thought. *"What would people say and think if I went to a shelter?"* I was too prideful to accept help, and I was too fearful of shattering my image to be transparent. So I did not let my advocate know that I needed more support. Short of giving me the normal speech I had heard my own mouth give so many times before, there was no additional help from my advocate. She did what she could, or rather, what I relayed I needed, but it wasn't enough. My main support lived thousands of miles away and although the telephone conversations were helpful, I needed a warm hug. I needed someone to help me navigate through the system. I needed someone to explain my options. I needed someone to tell me what I should ask my attorney and what I should expect in court. I needed to know certain things: do I even need to go to court, should I get an attorney? I needed to know the military process. I needed to know what would happen if I testified and what would happen if I didn't. I needed to know my rights and all my options. All the advocates were gone. I was truly alone. But I had spoken up and I was not going back into my prison of fear.

The journey of understanding abuse began for me when I made the decision not to be abused anymore. I knew conceptually and academically the cycle of violence. I was a great advocate for children in the foster care system. I had had many client who were victims of domestic violence but I didn't view my life as the same as theirs. I felt that because I was college-educated; my husband and I both had two master's degrees, we were not "the type of people" who had this kind of problem, and therefore I was not a real victim. I thought I did not appear like what my perception of the traditional victim looked like. That was the mask

I had gotten used to putting on daily. I had spent years talking myself into believing that I was fine and that the domestic abuse in my home was just normal fights that couples went through. I knew better. I knew what I experienced was power and control, that he had the control and the power and I had to bear the brunt of his mood swings. I knew I was a victim of a horrible cycle of violence. No, I wasn't hit on a daily basis, but when we did fight, he was physically aggressive. Every sign or symptom of domestic violence was present in my relationship. He was verbally and physically aggressive and abusive, I was isolated, he used the children as pawns, he used intimidation to control me and I afraid and too ashamed to speak up.

As I went through this process of transparency, I began thinking, of all those faces I had helped. I thought of my experiences with advocates and how I felt unsupported. And I also thought of how I had functioned as an advocate to my clients. I now identified with all those women I had aided, all those faces who had the courage to speak up. I knew I had joined this group of strong women - women who took their voices back. This decision to speak was not only the most difficult I had to make but also the saddest because the very thing I protected for almost fourteen years was the very thing I had to destroy by revealing the layers of secrets we had built. The very masks I had worn for years I now had to remove revealing the ugly truth. I realized that in moving forward I had to speak up and I had to shed years of secrets I had refused to acknowledge. I was afraid and I was alone, but somehow I knew I would be fine. Ok, Lord! Now what?

Chapter 2

NOW WHAT!

I awoke early in the morning and looked out my bedroom window. The air seemed crisp and cool, the morning was quiet. My mind was racing. Lord God, now what? What do I do now? My credit card was charged to the limit because my husband had paid his attorney fees as well as his jail bond for his arrest on it. All my accounts had been depleted and there was literally $2.00 in my checking account. What do I do? How am I supposed to trust God in this? And where was God?

I had always believed to have faith in God and that all things work out in the end, but this was a very hard pill to swallow. My faith had not been tested in such a manner before. As a couple we had saved quite a sum of money over the past ten years, living a debt-free life. When we first married we had a tremendous amount of debt, but my husband who was very business savvy, swore that we would be debt-free and in a surplus within five years, and we were. As bad as a spouse he was to me, he was an excellent financial provider. We had saved college tuition for our older son as well as savings for our retirement and other vacation and saving funds. We lived in a surplus the majority of our marriage. I didn't know how to live without the security of financial freedom so this zero balance had placed me completely out of my comfort zone. I knew there would be retaliation for speaking up, I could not believe that he would be selfish enough to take all the money; not just hurting me, but also the children.

Several days prior a mutual friend had warned me of my husband's appalling plan but I did not believe it would come to fruition. How were we doing? Of course I indicated that we were fine. I could not conceive that he would have left us with nothing. Those words now came back to me. This is what he meant. He intended to deliberately hurt me by depleting the funds. I began to seek counsel from my parents, and of course like parents who care about their children, they advised me to end the dysfunctional relationship permanently. Although they were not privy to the details of our marriage, as discerning parents and Christians they realized it was an unhealthy relationship and desperately wanted us to either seek help or go our separate ways for the children's sake. My closest friends who knew a little about our relationship were happy that I was finally getting "the help" they thought I needed. They knew we fought and that he was controlling, but I hadn't revealed the extent of our dysfunction. Their critique of our marriage left me feeling even more embarrassed and hurt. I didn't mind recognizing my husband for what he was, but I was very uncomfortable when my friends verbalized who he was. I didn't want to see him the way they did.

Some of our other friends had begun to distance themselves from us citing that they did not want to take sides. It was the most eye-opening experience that I had ever faced. Here I was bruised, beaten, broke and alone, and, the very people I had known for years had distanced themselves from me. I was devastated! Some voiced concern but stated the whole situation was uncomfortable for them, or they didn't know whom to believe. Or, they were unsure of what to do so they did nothing. I screamed in my head, *'Why would I destroy my family over a lie?'* But outwardly, I placed my familiar mask, smiling and stated that I understood.

I resolved to hate them all admitting they were never my friends to so easily forsake me. So, again, I was alone. Desperate for answers and support, I sought counsel from the only ones who were my constant – my parents. I also reluctantly sought counsel from the church. I had a dear friend, a senior Elder in the church who allowed me to vent without judgment; however, I had a love/hate relationship with church counseling. Although I was a licensed minister, although I believed that all things were possible with God, although many of my close friends were ministers and pastors, I had been very disappointed in how the church advised us. In short, I had grown weary of church counselors and church counseling. I had a strong distaste for clergy who were biased and inexperienced regarding domestic abuse. I had even greater disdain for pastors who misused Scripture giving the abuser even more power to control. I needed desperately to maintain my faith, but I was cynical of what counsel I would receive.

In the thirteen years of marriage, I had sought counsel from my churches before and it had proven to be a disaster. I recall one minister who counseled us together, even after I disclosed the abuse in the home. After one service, I went to the alter asking for prayer. I whispered my marriage needed help because my husband's explosive temper was scary and that we got into physical altercations in the home. The pastor listened keenly to me, and then asked me to come to his office after church so that he could talk to me. I recall his assistant leading me to his office. I had made an excuse to get away from my husband so that I could speak to the pastor in private. A few minutes later, to my disbelief the pastor and my husband walked in. I sat next to my husband and across from the pastor as he explained to my husband that I stated he had hit me. The pastor went on to say that he wanted to pray with us. I recall feeling the intense glare of my husband throughout the entire meeting. It was a look that only I could interpret. I knew what it meant when his jaw flexed. I understood his cold smile, and I was horrified but sat through the session quietly, denying any claim of abuse and minimizing fights and arguments that we had.

The pastor joined our hands and prayed for us to reconcile our marriage to God. At the end of the meeting not only was my husband vindicated through the counseling, but I was admonished for not being more supportive or submissive. After all, he was simply stressed about making the next rank so he lost his temper. The thirty-minute drive home seemed like a bare foot cross-country hike across a desolate barren plain. It was painful and emotionally grueling and long. I sat quiet and stone-faced as he yelled and belittled me for embarrassing him. The boys sat quietly in the back. At age 3 and 5 they had learned to be invisible when we fought. He didn't hit me that day, but I felt anxious each day waiting for the proverbial shoe to drop and I remained braced for a hit, a slap, a punch or a kick.

On another occasion, another pastor - a military chaplain no less - told me that as the mature Christian I needed to make my supplications known to God. When I divulged to him that our relationship had become toxic and that my husband was physically aggressive, he listened keenly, and then asked me if I was saved. I told him that I was. He asked me if my husband was saved, and I told him that I was unsure. Aware of the abuse I had disclosed, he told me to pray and fast for my husband's salvation and that my salvation could win him to God.

Another chaplain insisted on speaking to us together. After I came to this chaplain in confidence asking for marital help, he asked permission to speak with my husband alone. At first I was resistant thinking of the other times pastors had spoken to my husband. He then indicated that he wanted to talk to my husband to hold him accountable for his actions. I agreed thinking that being held accountable would result in a change of behavior and as a result improve marriage. My husband met with him one day in his office and came home with a few books on relationships.

The following week he asked to speak to both of us together. During the session, my husband cried and asked for forgiveness. He divulged that as a child he had witnessed his parents fight. This was news to me. I had no knowledge that there was discord in his parents' marriage. The chaplain asked me if I would forgive him. I felt trapped. I had seen this show of emotion before and I was very familiar with the tears and requests to be forgiven and I had grown weary of it. I was rude, defensive and aggressive. I was sick and tired of the charade. The chaplain gave me a book on forgiveness and brokenness and told me that it was time to forgive and build our new foundation. I was irritated. I didn't want to build anything, I had been here before; however, I reluctantly expressed that I would try again, but my heart was not in it. The chaplain ended the session stating that if I had forgiven him then we should move on and not to bring the topic up again. My husband was again empowered to be a bully because nothing changed. I found out later that he had lied about witnessing violence as a child. It was simply another ploy to manipulate me. He was still verbally and physically abusive. I had begun to stop caring. I had checked out emotionally.

Another minister advised me that marriage was not designed to make me happy, but rather to make me holy and that I should be content even in the abuse. I explained to him that I had become very unhappy in the marriage and that I needed some counseling, because I didn't recognize myself anymore. The minister explained that he did not condone the abuse, but I should pray during this season of marriage and wait for the season to change. I was livid. I had grown weary of the church and pastors. I did not trust their counsel, nor did I want it.

Through the years of counseling with pastors and ministers not one advised me to leave the abusive marriage - even after I admitted my husband had thrown my Bibles in the trash and instructed me not to play Christian music, read the Bible to the children or speak about God at all in the home. I recall being asked if he was unfaithful to me. When I stated that I did not believe he was, the session was dismissed as merely a couple's squabble. I was appalled; I was sick of clergy! I was sick of the "submitting wife" misinterpreted Scripture. I pointed out that the verse had two parts, which says the husband had to submit to God. The pastor thought I was defiant and told my husband that sometimes when women like me are too independent it makes it more challenging to submit. I did not want the advice of any clergy.

The more I thought of the past history of counseling, the more I didn't want to talk to a therapist either. During our mandatory counseling with family advocacy - where I minimized our toxicity - the therapist explained that she thought there was more going on, and I told her that I just want her and the situation to go away and that I regretted calling for help. She documented what I said and told me when I was ready to get help she would be ready to listen. But I never saw her again.

I was so accustomed to being let down by counselors that I had become acclimatized to handling the issues on my own. I thought if we talked with each other, then we would be able to solve our own issues without intervention. It was better than any other counseling that I had received. I needed to know what we were going to do, and how we were going to get past this for our children's sake. I didn't agree with my parents - I didn't think the marriage should be over. I began to think that perhaps we could get past this incident like we had in the past. Even after all I had been through, I was still strategizing of how we could reconcile. I was double-minded, because I needed to preserve the image we had built even after the lie of our life had been exposed. It was all I knew and it had become a normal way of living for me. I was unsure of leaving, because I didn't know the alternative. I was not yet willing to fully trust God although I said it verbally; I did not practice active faith.

I decided that I needed to talk to him. I was going to handle matters on my own and bring an end to this situation. I needed to see for myself if this was truly over. I had purchased a new cellphone, because he had destroyed my cell phone during our fight. He didn't recognize the number when he answered. His voice was hoarse, barely a whisper. He sounded alone, sad and afraid. My tears began to flow – *'Maybe we can make this work,'* I thought, as he sounded sad enough.

"Hello," I said softly. The phone went silent. I paused.

"How could you do this to me?" he started. "You realize this will ruin my career, you realize we will have to sell the house, you realize that I might go to jail, right?" he said coldly.

I stared blankly at the phone, and in a hoarse whisper I said, "You said you would never hit me again."

He interjected in a suddenly angry tone, "Don't call me anymore, I can't talk to you! You did this to us; remember that, you did this." Then the phone went silent.

After what seemed to be an eternity, the dial tone hummed softly jarring my mind back to reality. I sat back on my bed and stared at the reflection in the mirror. *'I did this? I ruined my life? Lord, now what? He won't talk to me; I have no idea how to proceed. Help me.'* I didn't know what else to do or how else to proceed. I looked at the mountain of paperwork I had reviewed from the hospital as well as the police department. I had several appointments I needed to attend. My tooth was broken, my eye glasses were broken, and my arm - still wrapped in a sling - continued to hurt with each movement. Furthermore, I had no money, the mortgage was due and I needed groceries. Now what Lord? What do I do?

As I sat uncertain of what to do, I looked at my sons asleep in my bed. The boys had been sleeping with me since the incident occurred. They were fearful every night. My ten-year-old had begun to wet the bed at night and my twelve-year-old had become a social recluse. He didn't smile, laugh, or even cry. He had internalized his feelings and refused therapy. He often curled up into my robe in my bed where he read his books until he fell asleep. I didn't know how I would take care of them.

I looked at myself in the mirror and right then I prayed a prayer that I believe changed the course of my life. *"Ok Lord, I give up, I give up, and I can't do this on my own, because I don't know what I need or how to move on, please take control. Shut my mouth when I need to be quiet and give me the words to say when it's time to speak up."* It was a simple prayer. It was my open heart. After I prayed I observed the pile of paperwork stacked on the nightstand. It was a pile from my advocate. There were pamphlets on counseling for children - as well as domestic violence - facts and statistics. I began to read through the information. Some of it I already knew because of my profession, but I read each line as if I had never seen it before. I read the impact witnessing violence had on children. I could see where it had already taken its toll on my sweet boys. I saw how it had taken its toll on my older son who had begun to avoid conflict, burying himself in schoolwork while rising to the top of his class. He became very passive, speaking in barely a whisper. My youngest, on the other hand, was his brother's antithesis. He was loud and boisterous very argumentative and disruptive. He also had several academic challenges with cognitive and processing delays. Additionally, he was emotionally under-developed. My eyes welled with tears, "I did this to them," I whispered hoarsely. "Lord, show me what to do," I cried. I prayed and cried laying hands on my children. I spoke Scripture over their lives stating that whatever plans the devil had for them, that they were null and void and that they would be prosperous because God had a purpose and a specific plan for each of them. I also began to speak to myself. I began to speak God's numerous promises, seeking Scripture to confirm his Words. That evening, I had spoken myself from a state of sadness to joy. It was time to move on.

Early the next morning I was ready to take some steps. I needed to talk with someone who could give me clear and concise directions. I needed someone objective. My parents were too angry. I needed a lawyer. I called several attorneys and began to visit each, retelling our life story and seeking counsel of how to proceed. "I only want to ensure the bills are paid and that the kids and I are taken care of until I get a job," I said to a young, well-dressed attorney sitting across from me in her lavish office. "I don't want a divorce, but I need to know what my rights are. I need to take care of my children," I explained to the beautiful, female attorney.

She sat back in her lush leather chair. "You need to go to the military; he is required to care for you" she indicated in a stern, unpleasant voice. "Kerry, you're a dependent and you are entitled to several rights that the military member has to adhere to, but I really want you to consider past the support. What do you want?" she asked looking squarely into my eyes. "From what I can see you are highly educated; you can start your life over if you want." I heard her, but she didn't seem interested in me. She stated her fee and concluded by closing her computer screen. "If you are interested in pursuing this further give me a call. But you should call his command first."

I decided to follow her lead; I called the command center and was given an appointment for that very afternoon. *'Ok,'* I thought, *'we can resolve this issue today and I will be able to move on. The bills will be paid, we can go to counseling and then we can maybe move to another installation. Then we can get back to life.'* It was a very naïve thought. I did not consider anything past getting support for the children, because I still had a very challenging time accepting the reality of my situation. Although I recognized the dysfunction, I was not yet thinking of a divorce. I was still planning a life together after what I had begun to call "the incident."

These incidents had occurred so many times before that it was second nature to me to go back to the home after a fight. We often fought verbally, sometimes it progressed to physical. We would give each other a day or two to cool off and then we celebrated that we were able to work through the issue. Then our life went back to normal until the next incident. What I had not realized at that time is that all along, we had been living in a cycle of domestic violence.

The cycle of violence in which we lived was a frantic roller coaster of emotional, psychological and physical abuse. We were often alright for long periods of time - weeks, months and even up to a year - with very little physical violence, but there was always verbal and emotional abuse. The name-calling and put-downs were consistent. There was a persistent undercurrent of toxicity. He made excuses for his behavior, often minimizing what he had done. I had learned to take the blame, downplay or minimize his part and also make excuses for his behavior. It was easier if I solved the verbal argument sooner. If I agreed to get along, it would sometimes prevent the argument from escalating to physical violence.

The arguments with which I had the most challenging times were those that involved a third party. If I spent too much time speaking with someone, an argument would ensue. No matter what I did or said to diffuse the situation, the argument was not one that I could easily solve. I needed to acknowledge my error. Sometimes if I turned the TV up too loud, laughed too loudly, or if my hair was not styled in a manner he liked, or dressed in a manner that was displeasing to him an argument would follow. I recall one incident where he physical cut a dress from my body. My girlfriends and I were going out to dinner to celebrate a birthday. I wore a little black dress that he believed was too sexy so he simply took a pair of scissors and physically cut the dress off my body. At the dinner I relayed the story to my friends who laughed uncomfortably at first, then expressed that the incident was concerning. I had been so used to the dysfunction that I didn't realize this incident was indicative of domestic violence. I minimized the occurrence citing that he was just playing, but inwardly I thought of what they said and I too became concerned. I was in a constant state of hyper vigilance and walked on pins and needles most of the time.

Situations which I attempted to avoid - because I knew they were triggers - were male friends, or any males communicating with me, or even looking at me. I made sure I kept a wide distance between me and any male, to show that I had no interest otherwise. Additionally, I made certain that I told him everywhere I was going and how long it would take before my return. I would attempt to ensure that no one called the house or stopped by, because he did not like my co-workers or my friends. I would verify the house was clean at all times and that the children played quietly or were out of his way when he came home. And most importantly, I would guarantee that any and all church activities or hobbies were limited, as he did not like me to be away from home. In short, I strived for his ideal perfection on a daily basis.

Although I knew these were all symptomatic of the dysfunction in a domestic violence case, I could not help myself. I had normalized the behavior to the point that I did not recognize that I was a victim. Whenever he was upset, he grew quiet, his jaw clenched and nostrils flared; but his silence spoke volumes. His eyes would dart throughout the house looking for anything out of place, so I became hyper-vigilant in reading his mind and his movements. Sometimes he would completely avoid me, even remaining silent in my presence for days – the silence was eerie, it was deafening. He only spoke to the children, often referring to me as he spoke to them, and would pass messages to me through them. It was always a scary, frustrating and uncertain time. I made sure not to bring any attention to his behavior because it would somehow become my fault. Whenever there was discord, I was blamed. It was often seen as my sensitivity, my inability to follow directions, my lack of attention to his needs, or my insensitivity and my inadequacies. I had accepted the fact that I was just inadequate for him.

During those tenuous times I paid particular attention to the children, because if the children did anything unpleasant I made certain to punish them immediately or conceal the incident from him; his punishment would be far worse than mine. I mostly concealed from him, because the boys didn't deserve punishments. The boys learned to be watchful as well. They were very obedient when he was at home as well as protective of me.

Because I did not understand the cycle of violence, I often became the peacemaker. I often covered his behavior from friends and family making excuses for his moods or his absence. I became the life of the party smiling and talking to ensure that everyone saw the wonderful team we were. Our act worked well, because he had moved up quickly in the ranks of the enlisted and was even promoted to an officer position. His arrest in Germany for domestic abuse was a distant memory because I had helped him conceal our dysfunction. We were well liked among our small circle and community. No one knew what happened behind our closed doors. Now here I was several years later sitting in a commander's office asking him to believe me, the spouse of his officer who had an impeccable record as a leader.

I sat at the commander's table feeling small and insignificant. I was intimidated but unafraid. He and another officer stood in their uniforms looming over me. They all stared at me blankly. There were two civilian women sitting in the office as well. I could tell they were talking about me by the way they whispered and hushed when I walked into their section. I was overwhelmed, feeling ashamed and embarrassed. I wasn't sure how to begin, so I simply asked for help. I explained that all the money was gone and I needed the military to help me by making my husband pay the bills. I didn't know then that this requested branded me as a "money hungry wife".

The commander's cool stare met my eyes from across the table. "Your husband said it was just a fight, but I hear you saying that this was more than a fight. Did you go to the emergency room? Do you have an advocate? Do you have an attorney?" He began to fire questions at me. I felt afraid and dumbfounded.

"No, I just want some help." I explained.

"Your husband says he wants a divorce."

My eyes welled with tears. "Divorce?"

"Your husband said that he caught you in an affair, that you began to hit him and that he was protecting himself."

My stomach leaped and I felt vomit drift to the surface, filling my mouth. I forced it back down and forced my tears back into the tear ducts. I refused to cry! *'He said what! Oh God help me,'* I cried inside, but I refused to let the tears flow in front of these strangers.

"No, that's incorrect," I stated softly. "I was not having an affair." I felt anger and heat and a sudden surge of energy. I stared the commander squarely in the face, "This was NOT the first incident of domestic violence, and no, I do not have an attorney. But I will be getting one. I just need to know how you can help me," I said calmly. "I have no money; he is in charge of the finances. I am new to the state, I don't know anyone. I need help." The young captain looked into my eyes. I could tell that something shifted. His expression changed.

"Ma'am, your husband is convinced you are having an affair, I suggest you get an attorney. There will be a comprehensive investigation into this matter. If you are having an affair, it will come out."

I couldn't contain it any longer. I was angry. Hot tears stung my eyelids then began to violently race down my cheeks. I had discovered spyware on my computer where my husband had been tracking my movements for the past month. I had been corresponding with a male friend who I dated in college. My husband had turned our correspondence into an affair. I was angry.

In my mind I began to scream *'I just wanted him to stop hitting me! I just wanted the yelling to stop, I just wanted the name calling to stop, I just wanted the controlling to stop, and I just wanted him to love me! No, I am not having any affair!'* But instead, I shook my head, "No, there is no affair. I was corresponding with a male friend, but there is no affair." I explained to the young captain that the young man I had corresponded with was currently deployed and that I had sent notes encouraging him. I further explained that he was married with a family and the only thing we rekindled was a long distance friendship and our love for dramatic arts.

The young captain hung his head. "Ma'am, I would encourage you to get an attorney. Your husband is obligated to take care of the children until your divorce is final.

I smiled mind-numbingly. "He's always accused me of an affair. If he saw me talking to you, he would be convinced that we were having an affair as well," I said dryly. "As far as he is concerned I've been having affairs since before we got married," I continued. I was tired.

"Ma'am, you should get an attorney."

"With what money?" I asked numbly. The young captain and the other officer left me for a few minutes.

The civilian woman brought me tissue and a cup of water. "This is always hard. How many times has your husband deployed?" the older woman asked.

"He's deployed once to a combat zone, but he's had several other Temporary Duty assignments," I stated.

"Well, it's hard on them, you know. You don't want to destroy his career honey, just take your time with this," she continued warningly.

I flinched. Was she serious? Did she see my arm in the sling? Did she see the swelling on my jaw and temple? I felt the heat rising under my collar. I was sick of this; I was sick of pretending that I was ok, I was sick of asking for help and sick of being sick of everything. I wanted to slap the taste from her mouth, "why is she in here", I thought. "I've given him thirteen years of time," I said coolly between clenched teeth. "Ma'am you don't know me, you don't know our history and you don't know how many times I've gone through this." "I understand you think you know my husband from your brief encounter with him the four months he has been on this installation; however, when you can say you have walked in my shoes the past thirteen years, then and only then you can talk to me about what I should, or shouldn't do!" I was livid, but I said it! I had spoken up. I finally said what was on my mind and it felt good to release it, but then I felt horrible for speaking so forcefully.

I exhaled heavily, and asked if the captain was coming back. The older woman stared into my eyes, and I matched her expression unflinching. Knowing that she had made a dire mistake in confronting me, she retreated back to her office with the other woman in tow. I was furious, and I was ready to leave.

I left the office, blinded by tears. I am not certain how I made it home, because I cried the entire eighteen miles from the installation to the house. I threw myself on my bed and wept aloud, "Lord, why! Why! Why am I going through this? I don't want a divorce, I just want peace; I just want to be happy. Lord, why am I going through this and what am I supposed to do?" I thought of what that woman said and the tears fell like streams soaking into my pillow. I screamed, beating my hands against the mattress, "Why? God what do you want me to do?" I crawled under my covers and prayed for the day to end. I had no energy. That day I did nothing, hoping tomorrow would be better.

The next day I again awoke early and looked out my window, hoping that my reality was actually a horrible nightmare. But the court documents across my dresser reminded me that it was not. I cried for the next two days and hid myself in my closet until my youngest son said these very poignant words to me, "Mommy, are you okay? I nodded through my tears. He eyed me pensively and said, "Mommy, did you pray?" I told him that I had. Then very confused he responded, "So why are you crying?" The innocence of a child is what shook me back to reality. It was the quickest and the best intervention I had ever experienced through the process of change. Why pray and worry? Why pray and fret? Why pray and cry?

Monday morning was another new day. I needed to talk to someone qualified to help me navigate these feelings. I needed to get this heaviness off. I needed to navigate the muddy waters of my emotions. I needed a therapist. I looked for the number the advocate had given me. I really didn't feel like sharing my heart with another stranger. I was tired of repeating the same thing over and over again. I felt sick. Soon after I made the appointment, I thought, 'Maybe I'll cancel. Maybe I will postpone it for a later date.' I sat at the edge of the bed and stared blankly into the mirror. I needed to get out of the house; I needed to be around another adult. I decided to go to the appointment.

I dressed carefully in fitted jeans and a simple monogramed shirt and sandals. I brushed my hair into a ponytail and applied a light powder to my face and topped it off with lip-gloss. After a quick check in the mirror again I headed out to see the therapist. Thirty minutes later I found myself seated across from an older woman with a kind face and, from the accolades and certificates on her wall, obvious years of experience. I was uneasy. The words of the woman in the captain's office came back to me, *'Don't ruin his career.'* I wasn't ready to share my thoughts or my feelings. I didn't want to shed any secrets. What if I told her everything that happened in the house? Would she notify child protective services? Could I lose my children? What about his military career? This was all we knew; I didn't want to ruin him, I just wanted help.

I had given up my career and opted to stay home for a while. *'Oh God, I don't have a job,'* I thought. I felt light-headed. I had begun to sweat. I needed to get out of there. *'I can't tell her anything,'* I thought to myself. *'She could destroy us. She could destroy my family.'* I looked around the room for a reason to leave. Nothing came to my head. She was talking, but I had no idea what she was saying. I watched her mouth move; her large teeth were pearly white and straight with a slight lipstick stain on the top front tooth. Her words were gibberish to me as all I could think about was getting home away from her judging eyes.

She had stopped talking and was looking directly at me. I blinked; what did she say? She handed me a stack of papers. *'What is this crap?'* I thought. *'I need to get out of here; I don't want to fill out papers.'* She began to talk again; she wanted me to complete the documents she handed me. My head was pounding, I looked over the papers. It was an assessment - a danger lethality assessment. *'Danger assessment?'* I thought, *'I'm not in danger. It was just a blasted fight, like many other fights we have had.'* I cussed in my head.

I looked at the form again. Yes, he hurt me. Yes, I am bruised. But this wasn't as bad as other fights. I thought I would answer a few questions and then leave, but first I would read the assessment. It was a checklist. I read the questions quietly to myself. Has he ever hit me – I checked yes. Has he punched me – I checked yes. Has he ever blamed me for his behavior – I checked yes. Does he have a weapon - I checked yes. Has he ever threatened suicide - I checked yes. Has he threatened to kill you – I checked yes. I began to feel very nervous. What was this woman going to do with this information? How could she hurt us? Can she help me? Would she help? What kind of help can she offer? How will this impact his career? My mind was reeling with questions.

She took the form from me and began to tally my responses. "17," she said, "your score is 17."

'Ok, 17. Did I fail? Did I pass?' I thought to myself, *'What does 17 mean?'* I cussed in my head, then quickly repented. *'Lady, hurry up!'* I

thought. She took her sweet time, quietly stacking the papers together. I began to drum my fingers on my thighs nervously. Then she quietly placed the stack of paper in her lap and said to me, "This tells me that you are in danger, you are more than likely to be killed in your relationship." She leaned close to me and explained the paperwork I had complete. The Danger Assessment is a tool used by the therapists which helps to determine the level of probability an abused woman has of being killed by her intimate partner. A score of fourteen is severe danger and eighteen and over represents a score of deadly danger. I had checked seventeen out of twenty **"YES"**!

I blinked back tears; I felt nothing for a moment, and then finally, I screamed inside. She looked at me contemplatively, because although I was screaming on the inside, my mask was quiet and composed. I knew how to manage my emotions in public; I had become an expert in covering. "Kerry, this is serious, do you understand?"

I nodded numbly. I choked back the tears. I could feel my eyelids filling with water. My mask was cracking; I was having a difficult time maintaining my composure. *'But you don't know him,'* I thought to myself, *'he's not a monster all the time. We have had good times when he wasn't angry. We have had great vacations. He's taken me to Paris and Portugal; we are well-*

traveled. We have a lot of money and we have master's degrees. We are not these people she is talking about.'

She talked for another twenty minutes, but I have very little recollection of what we talked about. Her mouth moved mechanically and her voice was a melodious lullaby that lulled me into absolute quiet. I knew she was speaking to me because I saw her mouth moving, but I have no idea what she said. The only sentence I recall was, "Maybe you can write your thoughts out, writing helps." I had checked out. I could not receive anything she had to say because I simply needed to get away. I kept a copy of the violence wheel as well as the assessment. Sitting in the car, I looked over them again and the top of the lethality sheet caught my attention.

SEVERAL Risk factors have been associated with increased risk of homicides of women and men in violent relationship. We cannot predict what will happen in your case but we would like you to be aware of the danger of homicide in situations of abuse and for you to see how many of the risk factors apply to you.

I carefully reviewed the assessment tool and my answers again. Then I looked at the domestic violence wheel and I could no longer ignore or pretend. **The truth was blinding. I was a victim of domestic violence and I was in** *danger!* I felt like the car was closing in on me and I desperately needed to get away. I drove behind a curtain of tears. I sat in my driveway with my head on my wheel and sobbed. Looking back, I believe she knew I needed to process alone.

Danger Assessment Tool Answers

Client Name_____ Date_____

Check yes or no next to each question.

1. ___Has the physical violence increased in severity or frequency over the past year?
2. ___Does he own a gun?
3. ___Have you left him after living together during the past year?
4. ___Is he unemployed?
5. ___Has he ever used a weapon against you or threatened you with a lethal weapon? _Was the weapon a gun?
6. ___Has he threatened to kill you?
7. ___Has he avoided being arrested for domestic violence?
8. ___Do you have a child that is not his?
9. ___Has he ever forced you to have sex when you did not wish to do so?
10. ___Does he ever try to choke you?
11. ___Does he use illegal drugs? (street drugs, uppers, or amphetamines, "meth, speed, spice, cocaine, crack or mixture")

12.____Is he an alcoholic of problem drinker?

13.____Does he control most or all of your daily activated? **For instance:** does he tell you who you can be friends with, when you can see your family, how much money you can use or when you can take the car?

    a. __Check here if he tries but you don't let him

14. ____Is he violently and constantly jealous of you?

15.__Have you ever been beaten by him while you were pregnant?

    a. __If you have never been pregnant by him check here__

16.__Has he ever threatened or tried to commit suicide?

17.____Have you ever threated or tried to commit suicide?

18.____Does he threaten to harm your children?

    a. ____Does he ever threated to have you children taken away from you?

19.____Do you believe he is capable of killing you?

20.____Does he follow or spy on you, leave threatening notes or messages, destroys your property or call you when don't want him to?

21. ___ Does he prevent you from gaining employment?

22. ___ Does he minimize the abuse, deny the abuse or place blame on you?

Domestic Violence Wheel

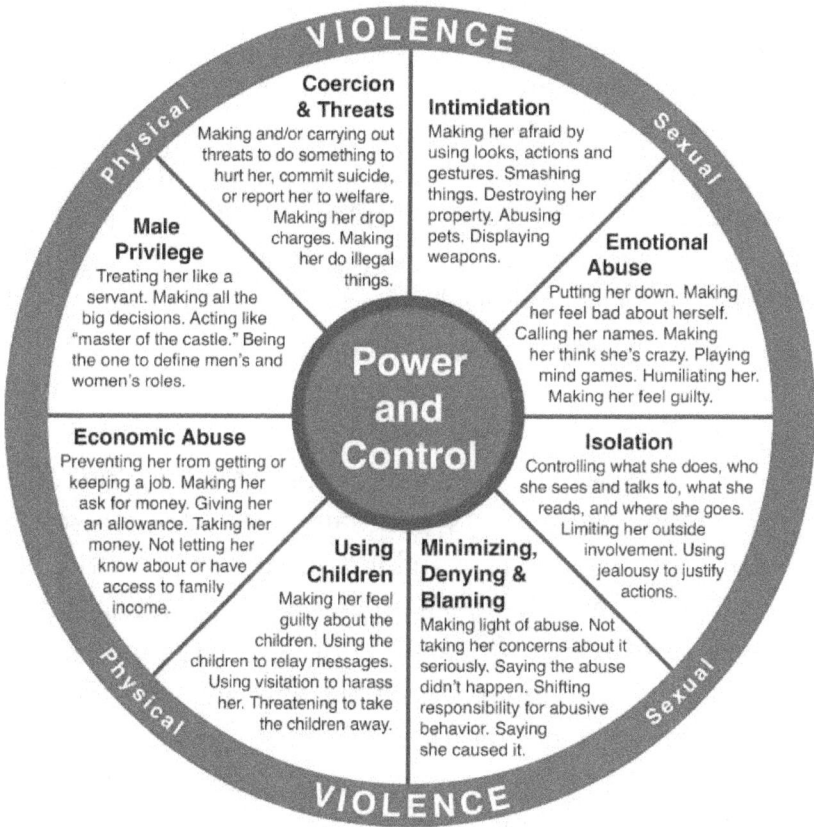

VIOLENCE

Coercion & Threats
Making and/or carrying out threats to do something to hurt her, commit suicide, or report her to welfare. Making her drop charges. Making her do illegal things.

Intimidation
Making her afraid by using looks, actions and gestures. Smashing things. Destroying her property. Abusing pets. Displaying weapons.

Male Privilege
Treating her like a servant. Making all the big decisions. Acting like "master of the castle." Being the one to define men's and women's roles.

Emotional Abuse
Putting her down. Making her feel bad about herself. Calling her names. Making her think she's crazy. Playing mind games. Humiliating her. Making her feel guilty.

Power and Control

Economic Abuse
Preventing her from getting or keeping a job. Making her ask for money. Giving her an allowance. Taking her money. Not letting her know about or have access to family income.

Isolation
Controlling what she does, who she sees and talks to, what she reads, and where she goes. Limiting her outside involvement. Using jealousy to justify actions.

Using Children
Making her feel guilty about the children. Using the children to relay messages. Using visitation to harass her. Threatening to take the children away.

Minimizing, Denying & Blaming
Making light of abuse. Not taking her concerns about it seriously. Saying the abuse didn't happen. Shifting responsibility for abusive behavior. Saying she caused it.

Physical · Sexual · Physical · Sexual

VIOLENCE

It had become too real and too overwhelming to process with a stranger. After what seemed like an eternity, I finally picked my head up from my steering wheel but I couldn't stop thinking of the wheel and danger assessment. I could see the pattern of our life on that wheel. I could see the escalation, the honeymoon periods and also the outbursts on the wheel. I knew what she said was true. I knew I needed help, but I wasn't ready to admit that I had failed to a stranger. I wasn't ready to say I was wrong. I wasn't ready to say that my life was a lie; especially to someone I had just met.

I tossed and turned most of the night reliving the last fight, "the incident", which was the catalyst for my current distress. I thought of the many fights we'd had over the years. I thought of my husband flipping the black leather couch over while I was pregnant twelve years prior. The assessment asked if he ever struck me while pregnant; that question brought a flood of memories back. I was pregnant with our first son and because I had confided in my cousin about the pregnancy, he became enraged, punching the walls and closet door and forming large holes. I explained to him that I simply needed a friend to talk to, and he flipped the couch over pinning me beneath. The violence continued throughout the pregnancy and seemed to get worse as the pregnancy progressed. I confided in my mother-in-law, who instructed me to stop arguing with him. She saw the holes in the walls and the doors and counseled me about being quiet when he was moody.

I thought of him dragging me down the stairs by my hair while the children hid under their beds (I could still see their little faces frightened as they ran to their rooms). I thought of the closed-fist punches to my back and face. I thought of him flipping our king-size mattress over, pinning me beneath while he stomped on the mattress. I thought of him grabbing me and slamming me into a wall, preventing me from going to the children who were crying and hiding under their beds. I thought of him shouting at the boys and yelling obscenities to them. I thought of him throwing my Bibles away because he did not want me attending church anymore or reading it to the boys. I thought of him telling the boys that I was a whore and I was worth nothing. I thought of the clicking sounds of his gun as he cleaned his weapons at night after a fight. I had no more tears to weep. I knew I needed help. I knew I had to get out. I now understood what I needed to do.

That night I decided that it was critical to shed the secrets. I needed to get out before he kills me. This was not fixable. I decided to hire an attorney to help me navigate the muddy waters of domestic violence. It was after midnight, but I decided to call and leave a message on the voicemail to one of the attorneys I had spoken with before I changed my mind. As I dialed the number I prayed, "Lord, I don't want revenge. I don't wish to destroy him. Search my heart; anything that is not of you, remove it please. Lord, help me to tell the truth as it happened and not as I see it. Lord, guide my tongue and thoughts to be truthful rather than right. Lord, remove anger and malice from my heart and spirit; give me the joy of my salvation. Lord give the counselors ears to hear and eyes to see the truth. Lord, have your way."

That night I slept peacefully for the first time since our separation. My mind was made up, and I knew God was with me. I was no longer double minded; I needed to move forward no matter how hard it would be and no matter where it led me. I needed to break my silence.

CYCLE OF VIOLENCE WHEEL

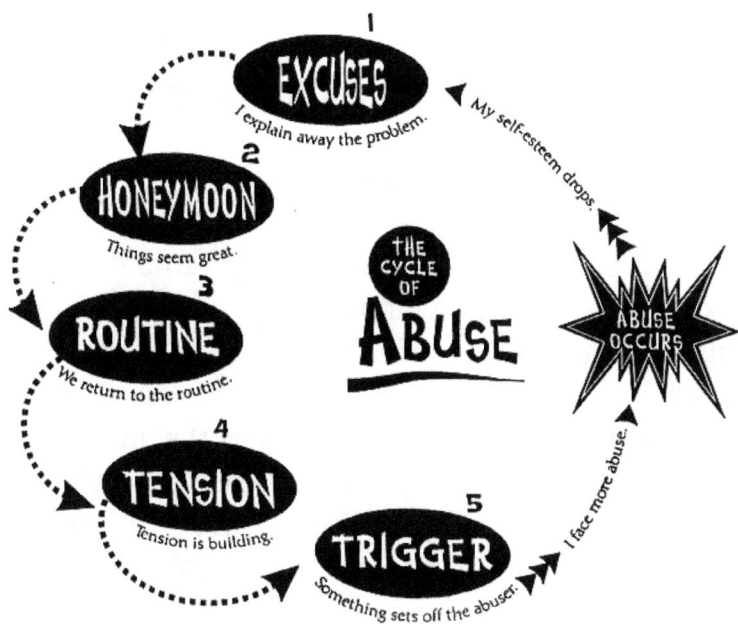

THE CYCLE OF ABUSE

1 **EXCUSES** — I explain away the problem.

2 **HONEYMOON** — Things seem great.

3 **ROUTINE** — We return to the routine.

4 **TENSION** — Tension is building.

5 **TRIGGER** — Something sets off the abuser.

My self-esteem drops.

I face more abuse.

ABUSE OCCURS

Chapter 3

BREAKING THE SILENCE

Going through something traumatic is exhausting, terrifying and lonely; however, it can also be a time of reflection. I am able to look back on my life and see where God was pruning me for His good. I can also see the mistakes I made because of my own choices. I can see where the enemy of my soul - Satan - used bad experiences to make me feel ashamed and fearful. The Bible says that the devil is like a roaring lion seeking whom he may devour. I felt this attack for very long periods of my life. I carried the blame for what my abusers did to me because of guilt and shame, and that resulted in me making poor choices as a teenager and young adult. I believed the devil used the bad that happened to me to confuse and confine me. Because I did not have a sound foundation in Christ as a young person, I made bad choices. Many of those choices led me to my abusive husband. I stayed in an abusive relationship because I had lost my sense of self. I was too prideful to leave. Because I didn't know who I was, and I had very little self-esteem, I accepted poor treatment although intuitively I knew I deserved better.

After leaving the therapist I could not stop thinking and processing all I had been going through. She had sparked my desire to write. Writing had been a passion from an early age, but I had not written anything personal in years. I needed to get the thoughts out of my head. I could not stop thinking about how I had allowed this to happen to me. I did not ask to be beaten, but I saw a lot of the warning signs and ignored them. Early in the relationship he would become upset for what I thought were silly reasons. He felt my friends took up too much time, or he did not know who I was talking to, or sometimes he just required my undivided attention at the most inopportune times. I instinctively knew his behavior was abnormal, but I thought I could fix it. I thought I could help him trust more.

After we married and the behavior continued, I thought I could protect my children because they did not physically see the violence or they were too young to know what was going on. I was wrong on all counts. I could not fix him, and I could not fix our problems without help. I could not protect the children from him unless they were away from him. And moreover, they were affected. They did not have to physically see any of our fights, but the aftermath of the physical assault and the evidence of the broken glass debris had a definite impact on their well-being. I noticed they became clingy after outbursts. My older son retreated to his books. Initially I was quite pleased that he had taken such an interest in reading, but as the years passed I noticed he preferred books to social interaction. It had become his security. It was his safe place. My younger son was quite opposite. He became defiant, clingy and had developed several learning challenges. He needed a lot more attention from me. He cried often and was very sensitive to loud noises. Moreover, he refused to engage with his father.

The next time I went to the therapist I began to disclose what my children had witnessed. I needed someone to whom I could vent and I needed to know how I could help my children. I felt tremendous guilt for exposing them through the cycle of violence. I needed to know how I could help my boys overcome the trauma of what they saw.

After listening to me, the therapist referred me to an excellent play therapist. During that time the children had begun visits with their father. They often returned home upset, retreating into their rooms. I discovered their father would try to persuade them to live with him by telling them that I was sleeping with other men. Of course this was not only confusing and hurtful to the children, but it devastated their self-esteem because they took on the responsibility of defending their mom. I realized that in order to help the boys, I had to be whole. I had to continue the process of shedding my anger and resentment.

My therapist asked me if I kept a journal. She sensed that I was extremely angry and thought writing would be therapeutic for me. I explained to her I had not written in a while, but that writing was one of my favorite pastimes. She encouraged me to write. "Kerry, write everything you can remember."

My laptop was destroyed - broken in half from our last fight - so, I pulled out a legal pad and I began to write. The first line read: "This is not how I imagined my life." The words began to flow like water from a faucet. When I stopped writing, it was over an hour later and I had written more than five pages. I had recalled every incident during the marriage. The weight of the memories overwhelmed me, my heart rate began to escalate, my palms became clammy and moist, my throat felt dry, and I was experiencing breathing problems. I began to sob. As the tears left my body, I felt a surge of energy that I had not felt before. I wanted to talk. I wanted to break the silence. I needed to use my voice again, and I wanted to be heard.

A few days later, I sat across from my new attorney. My stomach churned and my heart leaped. I was ready, but I was terrified. As I recounted the events of the night in question, my attorney listened keenly. He sat back in his chair and asked, "Do you have a counselor?"

I blinked. "A counselor?"

"Ma'am, the level of domestic violence you have experienced, I believe, warrants some ongoing therapy. I am not a therapist, but from my years of practicing law and working with victims of violence, I hope you would consider seeing someone."

My heart smiled. He appeared to care. He was the right attorney for me. "Can you tell me what I need to do to file for divorce? I don't want to destroy my husband, or his career. I simply want to move on with my life; I know we cannot move on together." It had begun. I signed the paperwork for divorce admitting that the terms for divorce were spousal abuse. My silence was broken; but, so was I.

The decision to divorce my husband was not one that was easy. It was a decision that I made out of necessity for not only my sanity, but also the future of the two boys. This was a decision that I had thought about on and off for two years prior, but it was something I was very fearful of. I didn't want to give up the life I had become accustomed to or the image of the happy family that we had built. I was fearful of what people would say. I was fearful of the unknown. I was fearful of being on my own. I knew the boys had seen years of dysfunction and violence between their parents, and I desperately needed to let them know that domestic violence was not okay; that their mother and every woman should be treated with respect.

I had stayed thirteen years for the belief in family and it was a bad decision; it exposed my children to an unhealthy relationship. Now I needed to leave to give them the opportunity for a healthier family life. Even after I had begun the process of the divorce, I often tried to rationalize reasons not to go through with it, not because I loved my husband and wanted to make our marriage work, but rather for the sake of my children. I vacillated back and forth; was it the best decision for them? I read statistics about young African American boys in a single parent home and I was fearful. But I knew in my heart I could not go back and that going back was not in their best interest.

It may seem heartless to say that I didn't love my husband; I thought I did. But as the weeks passed on, I realized what I thought was love, was fear and familiarity. In fact, my marriage had been dying for several years. We cared for each other because of the long history we had together, but there was no love or resemblance of love. You cannot love someone the way God intended love to be if you are in constant fear of them. Love is not supposed to hurt. The reality was I wanted to love him, but I feared him more. Even when he was not being physically abusive, there was a constant state of fear because his mood could change at any time from jovial to sullen to enraged. Any resemblance of love we had had dissipated years prior. It was replaced by a mutual desire to maintain a lifestyle.

Even after realizing that my relationship was devastatingly dysfunctional, toxic and dangerous, I was fearful of moving on. I began to attend counseling with an Elder who ministered the Word of God to me. For the first time I was told that his abusive behavior was not God's plan for me and that His plan for me is to prosper not harm me. My Christian counselor ministered to me that God had a plan for me and that my beginning does not determine my ending. Although I was still fearful of the unknown life as a single parent, I knew God was in control. I recalled the counseling years prior with a military chaplain, he had explained the statistical data to us regarding young men who are raised without a father. He had encouraged me to remain in my marriage because he said many young men from broken homes weren't successful in college, or they engaged in juvenile delinquent behavior. I was very fearful of my children not getting the best, so I stayed. A pastor once said to me that as the mature Christian it was my duty to stay and pray and fast for my family; that if I were to leave, my children would be the ones who would suffer. These messages from church leaders and chaplains were not admonishments to him, but rather to me. I had to protect my children, even if it meant that I stayed in an abusive relationship. But now, this man of God was telling me the antithesis. That yes, God hates divorce, but God loves me and it is not his plan to see me hurt. I believed him, but I also questioned God's plan. I had a lot of hurts in my life, did God see those hurts and what was His plan?

As I began to journal different incidents of domestic violence in my marriage, I pondered on the trauma my children may have witnessed and how it would impact their lives later on. I knew very well how childhood trauma often impacted decisions made. As I stated earlier a lot of my decisions as a young adult was due to past childhood trauma. My therapist asked me to journal as much as I could recall from my childhood. I didn't want to recall those experiences. Those fears I had buried years ago, and I didn't want to revisit them; but I knew that I needed to address my past in order to move forward

Often time we try to move on without acknowledging how we got to a certain point. I had done that. I had ignored my past hurts. As I began to journal traumatic events in my childhood, I spoke with my therapist and realized that some traumatic events had led me to my husband. Because of my innate self-hate, I entered and remained in a relationship that was abusive. Somewhere within myself I had accepted that I should be treated lesser than who I was. Somehow I had accepted a negative sense of self. I needed to revisit my childhood; I knew that in order to move forward I had to go back to where my self-hate began.

Going Back To Move Forward

I grew to hate the smell of Guinness but I did not recall why until I began to journal. My earliest recollection of child sexual abuse was age 4. I wore a green jumper with green lace ribbons in my hair. We visited a friend of the family who I called "Auntie". My mom was inside chatting and laughing with the women while I played on the front porch. My "auntie's" husband, Uncle Fagan, was lying in his hammock drinking a Guinness. Uncle Fagan and Auntie were not biologically related to me. They were family friends who were very close to my mom. My uncles and my Papa, the men in my life, were kind and gentle souls who had never harmed me.

The smell of Guinness was familiar; my Papa often drank the same drink. But, this uncle was not like my uncles or my Papa. He did not have a melodic laugh like they did, he had a frightening laugh. His touch was not warm and safe, I did not like him. I recall sitting on the floor playing with marbles when he called me to come to his hammock. He asked me to give him a hug. I didn't want to hug him; he was fat and sweaty. "Be a good girl and give uncle a hug," he urged me. I remember going to the hammock reluctantly hugging him as he swung his legs over the side to scoop me into his arms. He hugged me and began to feel my bottom and then my crotch; he called it "tickling me". I didn't like his tickle and I didn't like the way he touched me. I felt scared, but I wasn't sure why. Every time we visited Auntie, Uncle tickled me. Sometimes when I wore a skirt or dress he would try to tickle me under my clothes. I fought him. I recall telling him I didn't like his tickling and I would hit him to prevent him from touching me. One day Uncle tried to pull my panties down and I bit him. I remember he laughed at me, and then told me not to tell anyone because my mommy would be mad at me for being bad. He would offer me candy and treats, but I was defiant; I recall telling him, "You're bad, I'm not bad."

I told my mom I didn't like the way Uncle tickled me. I told her that Uncle was bad, but she didn't say anything; she didn't tell him to stop tickling me. She laughed and said, "Uncle is not bad." I was crushed. Maybe I was bad. Maybe Uncle was right.

Years later, as a teenager, I realized that the tickling, touching my private parts under my clothes, was sexual abuse. He had groomed me and exposed me to adult behavior that I was unprepared for; he had groomed me for the next perpetrator to abuse me. Although I had told an adult, because I could not describe the behavior, and I used the word "tickling", which was a common play with children, my mother did not comprehend that this act was not the normal playful act, but that I was being abused. This act is considered grooming. Grooming is a predatory act where the abuser is deliberately establishing a bond with a child to lower the child's resistance. When a child is groomed it is more likely that the child will be abused by another abuser more easily.

For a very long time I was upset and confused but I never quite understood why. I vacillated between anger and restlessness as a child. I had a hard time sitting still; I often daydreamed wishing I was far away. The abuse left me with a lot of self-doubt which had a long-lasting effect on me emotionally. I was fearful of men. I was defiant and I often became agitated, which over time was interpreted as a behavior problem. I was inattentive and fidgety because I felt uncomfortable in my skin. Although I did the right thing by telling my mom that I didn't like visiting Uncle Fagan, she didn't understand why. As an adult, I then understood why my mother had reacted the way she had. She had no knowledge or understanding of abuse. This was not a topic of discussion in 1979 and information about abuse was not readily available for parents. In addition, my mom had lived in that same home, with Auntie and Uncle Fagan for several years without incident. She had no idea and no reason to mistrust him.

Unfortunately, the door had been opened. I had become vulnerable to abuse. After that day, whenever we visited I sat inside with the women. I refused to play on the front porch. I refused to let Uncle touch me, but no one noticed. I don't recall when the visits stopped, but I know that I made certain not to be left alone with Uncle Fagan. I had begun to learn how to protect myself. Although Uncle Fagan never touched me again, I could not forget what he did; it was forever engrained in my head and I hated him. He left me with the thought that something was wrong with me.

A few years later, my mother had migrated to America leaving me with my biological aunt and her family. I was very confused and lost when my mother left. I did not understand that I would not see her for a long time. I also didn't understand that my mother left to make a better life for us in America. She couldn't take me with her and at the time she thought she was doing the best thing for me. I recall first being thrilled to be with my cousins. As an only child, the prospect of playmates on a daily basis was exciting. As the months passed by I began to miss my mom. I loved my aunt, my uncle and my cousins, but I needed my mother.

I had always been a rough-and-tumble kind of girl. I loved climbing trees and playing in the dirt. I could out-run and out-spit any boy. I enjoyed competing with my cousins as well as any other child in the neighborhood. One day another cousin came to live with us temporarily. He was older than all of us. Of course being a tomboy I wanted to hang with my older cousin and he took note of that. We often wrestled, climbed trees and played on the beach. One day we wrestled and I began to feel uneasy. He reminded me of Uncle Fagan. He was very different when he wrestled with me. I didn't like it, I didn't like him. I recall being left alone with him and he wanted to wrestle and tickle me the same way Uncle Fagan had. I flinched. I didn't like the way he tickled me, but I didn't react. Who would I tell this time?

I recall him taking me by the hand and leading me to a room stating he wanted to show me another game. He opened his pants and showed me his private parts. I didn't know what to do. I recall being confused, afraid and sad. I wanted my mom. For the next year, my cousin abused me all the while stating that there was no one to tell. No one would believe me. I was known for doing things that stirred trouble; I was loud, aggressive and argumentative. I believed him. No one would believe me. They would think I was bad. So, I remained silent.

One day, during an encounter with my cousin, I felt a surge of anger. I recall grabbing a pencil and angrily stabbing into his flesh as he touched me. I spat on him venomously challenging him. He grabbed my hands and slammed me against the wall. I stood straight and glared at him saying, "I'm not afraid of you." As I said those words, I gained more strength. I pushed him away and began to walk away from him. What happened next I never spoke of until years later. I recall running all the way home to my aunt's house. I was angry; I was hurt.

I wanted to go home to my mom. I wanted her hugs; I didn't want to be here any longer. I hated everyone around me. I was sinking quickly and I needed a life saver. My aunt saw a change in me. She saw that I had become angry. I didn't want to play anymore. One evening she said, "You're going to see your mommy in America." I was overjoyed. America, no one would touch me in America. I was ready to go.

Three months later I was an American child, but I had changed. The last day spent with my older cousin had left me distorted. My innocence was not only lost, but my childhood had been stripped from me. I thought of nothing else and found adjusting to American lifestyle very difficult. I didn't understand the culture, the clothes or the lingo. I was lost. I had a difficult time making friends and I trusted no one. I was happy to be back with my mom and my dad, but I was unhappy. I was unable to process my unhappiness, so I buried myself in books and my writing. I wrote plays and short stories and poetry to pass the time, but I never rekindled the childhood I once enjoyed. I also had become angry at God.

Years later, I graduated from high school and I began to date in college. I didn't date during high school; primarily because my parents did not allow it, but also, I had a hard time trusting men. When I began to date in college, I met someone who was kind, gentle and absolutely hilarious. We immediately developed a close friendship. For the first time in my life, someone didn't want to hurt me. Our relationship lasted a few months and then, like most young adult relationships, it fizzled off. A few months later I met the man who had become my first love. I was in love with the idea of being in love. So when I met this tall, dark chocolate man with a twinkle in his eye, I was smitten. We did everything together and we thought, well, I thought, we would spend the rest of our lives together until I became ill at school and I was brought home.

Within three hours of leaving the hospital emergency room, I was back home in Maryland. My things would be shipped from college. Within the next six months, my relationship had come to a sudden end with no contact from my love. I was devastated and crushed. As the months passed on, I realized that the relationship was over. I fell into a depression, and then desperation. I needed to rekindle the feeling of someone loving me. I wanted to love someone again.

That fall I enrolled in the local state university and moved into the dormitory. Although my goal was focused on completing college, I was lonely and I was sad. I hung a picture of my love over my bed and wished for the day we would reunite with each other. Then one day, there he was; A new attraction, Mr. Tall and Light-skinned. I was immediately attracted to his confidence. We became fast friends. We spent hours talking and laughing and I was smitten for the second time in my life. I had gained the friend I so desperately needed. I needed someone who adored me, who showered me with affection and attention, who wanted me to be the most important in the world to them. And he was that.

Unfortunately, what I didn't know was that his love for me was a dangerous beginning.

Everything that happened to me in my childhood exposed me to being vulnerable to meeting my abusive husband. Uncle Fagan's abuse was the door that opened the way for my cousin to abuse and rape me and the untimely ending of the relationship in which I learned to trust. Those events were the catalysts to my negative self-image, poor self-esteem and vulnerability.

I always knew and felt intuitively that God had a purpose and a plan for me. I wrote stories and poems and plays, but there was always a feeling of inadequacy and self-doubt because of the abuse I had experienced. I attended church, and even operated in ministry but felt a deep anger and confusion toward God, because I felt he had abandoned me as a child. I didn't understand the purpose for my pain. I often thought, *'Why me? Why so much pain?'*

The most dangerous behavior is self-destructive behavior. I was never promiscuous; I was too afraid to be. I never abused substances; again, I was too afraid to do that. My self-destructive behavior was trying to be perfect. It was not admitting to my feelings, but rather wearing a mask and pretending that everything was ok. I had become steel. I had become a people pleaser to the detriment of self. Despite the abuse that occurred in my childhood, I can say I had a rather pleasant childhood. I had a loving family and I felt loved. But, I didn't know who I was as a woman, as an individual, so I became trapped in the idea of what I thought love was.

For years I had tried to make my marriage work, doing whatever deemed necessary to me. If my husband didn't like my hair, I changed it. He hated my braided hair, so I made certain to wear my hair long and straight. If he didn't like my weight, I adjusted; I made certain to remain the size he liked. If he didn't like my clothes, then I changed. I lived for him rather than God and consequently I could no longer recognize myself. I had given up on being happy.

After years of going to couples counseling for different abusive events in our marriage, I had begun to doubt that there would be a change in our relationship. I had become indifferent. I could no longer muster the energy to be angry. I didn't feel, nor did I reciprocate, a loving relationship. We were excellent at pretending and masking, but deep inside I was empty, lonely and dying. As my marriage began to decline, I began to recall the days when I felt the happiest. They were days with my first love. That was where I made a critical mistake, a poor choice.

I had become lonely and unhappy. Whenever we stray away from where God intends us to be, we find ourselves where we ought not to be. Like Eve had wandered off from Adam and found herself under the tree of temptation lured by the serpent, I, too, had found myself wandering off from my husband. I had begun to communicate my dissatisfaction and loneliness to a male friend, my first love who I found through mutual friends. Before I knew what was happening he had become my number one confidant and close friend. Again, the devil in his cunning knows exactly what appeals to us. He knew that I was lonely and unhappy and he knew that the reconnection with my first love would draw me in. Although over 16 years had passed by, we spoke like we had just seen each other the day prior. The innocence in which our reconnection began became blurred. He reminded me of a time in which I was happy, free and fun and I desperately wanted to find that girl again. Rather I had become sullen, sarcastic and aloof. I hung on his every word, each day eagerly waiting for any communication from him. I needed to feel; I needed to feel anything but this lonely existence I had learned to accept. This opened a dangerous door because the only safety and security I felt was with this rekindled friendship. I had become emotionally dependent on another man. I didn't seek out an affair nor would I classify our friendship as an affair. But our relationship was one that had become very important to me; more important than this abusive relationship with my husband. My friend was thousands of miles away but emotionally he was with me all the time. I knew in my heart that his friendship had replaced my husband but it was not an affair as affairs are classified; however, perhaps in hindsight, might not have been the best choice.

I had a problem and my husband sensed that I no longer cared about him. The problem was that I was tired of faking, tired of pretending that we were happy and, most importantly, I was tired of being unhappy.

I looked up from what seemed liked hours of writing. I sat in the middle of the king-size bed and began to read what I had written shedding tears for all the secrets that had kept me in an emotional bondage. The secret things I had kept for years were now written on paper, and it was real. I had been abused, raped, and beaten - and I didn't die. I had been angry for so many years while wearing a smiling mask that I didn't expect to feel the freedom of releasing the weight of secrecy. "I need to let you go," I whispered to myself out loud. At that point I heard the Holy Spirit say, "Release them. Release your abusers to me; the weight you have carried is preventing you from soaring." It was 10 pm, but I picked up the telephone and called my husband; whether he listened or not I didn't care. I dialed the number with renewed strength. "I forgive you, I'm releasing you," I said when he answered the phone. "I am sorry I hurt you by communicating with my male friend. I cannot be with you anymore because we are not healthy for each other." There was nothing else to say except "goodbye." I breathed a deep breath when I hung up the phone. No tears; I had no tears, just fresh air.

I decided to continue the process by writing in bold letters on a sheet of paper I had taken from my printer, "I forgive you Uncle Fagan" and "I forgive you cousin". I then said the words out loud, "I FORGIVE YOU, I AM RELEASING YOU." The act of writing and then uttering those words were restorative. I took a deep breath then took the pieces of paper to the fireplace. As I lit the paper I said a quiet prayer. "God forgive me for holding onto this weight. Forgive me where I was wrong, I release them to you. Show me how to live free," and then I walked away leaving the ashes behind.

The time of mourning was over. I had vowed to leave the ashes where they were and to begin to live again with the promise of the new beginning of joy. I was ready for happiness. It had taken me almost four months after our last domestic abuse incident and five months of counseling to get to this point. Nine months later, I could see my bright future. I had to recognize for myself that I needed to let go in order to move forward. I had shed my secrets and it was time to begin again. The most amazing thing about releasing issues to God is the sensation of a heavy weight being lifted. It is complete brokenness and wholeness all in one. I was ready to be restored.

Chapter 4

RESTORED

Completely broken, there was nothing else to write, nothing else to tell. All the secrets had been shed, layer by layer. I sat looking at myself as if for the first time, transparent and free. The weight of the skeletons in the cupboard had been loosed. The guilt and shame that I had carried for so many years like shackles were released. There were no more tears to discard, my tear ducts were barren, my head pounded and my body was weak. I finally looked up into the eyes of my therapist. She appeared as exhausted as I as she continued wearily observing my face for a sign. I exhaled releasing my shoulders as I slowly leaned back sinking into the soft leather loveseat. I had written fifty-two pages and I had told her every word, like a vulgar plague expelled like sputum from my pen. I had released the weight from childhood, adolescence and adulthood. I felt weak. My heart which once pounded in my chest had regulated back to a soft thud. Every burden was released.

I looked up at my therapist with heavy eyelids. She continued to observe me quietly, I could not accommodate her; there was nothing. I had nothing to share. There was absolutely nothing she could say or do, but continue to stare at me contemplatively. We sat in silence for what seemed to be an eternity, but in reality only a minute or two. I knew then that I needed to return to the joy of my salvation. My therapist had taken me as far as she could. She had listened; she had helped empower me, now it was up to me to live again. It was time for me to take charge of my life and rebuild. I needed to regain the peace of mind that I once had so long ago. I desperately needed to leave. I needed to be alone. Quickly gathering my purse, I bade my therapist goodbye knowing that I had no intention of returning. I left the therapy session exhausted and headachy.

I called my victim advocate as I drove, to thank her, knowing that she, too, had taken me as far as she could. She had left me several messages checking on me. Although I appreciated her efforts she couldn't help me. I needed to take this walk alone. She had introduced me to a plethora of resources. She had listened while I vented and she allowed me to make my own decisions. I needed to take the next step. It was my turn to fly with unclipped wings. I arrived home from my short drive and immediately went to my room. I kicked off my heels, loosened my ponytail allowing my hair to fall messily around my face. I climbed into my bed fully-clothed, pulled the covers up to my neck and slept in peaceful slumber. This was not a nap of escape or depression, this was relief and release. This was absolute peace. I slept until I heard the chime of the front door. It was now 3:00pm and the boys were home. I had slept most of the day away.

The next morning I awoke with new vigor, and new purpose. After walking my younger son to school, I returned to the house, but first paused at the rose bushes in the front yard. Every day I had walked past the rose bushes which lined the driveway, but today each tree, bush and shrub seemed to have new purpose and new meaning to me. I noticed the rose bush had outgrown its form and it had begun to look rather untidy. Without thinking I reached in to arrange a few branches which spilled over into an azalea bush. Before I knew it, a thorn had not only pricked my finger but it had torn my flesh. I jumped back and applied slight pressure to my hand.

Irritated, I left the untidy bush and went inside to make my breakfast. As I sipped my juice I caught a glimpse of the Band-Aid on my hand and thought of the rose bush. It needed pruning. I needed to trim the hedges to bring it back to its beauty; but, first I needed gloves and pruning shears. I smiled to myself as I recalled the prayer I had prayed several weeks prior. I had asked God to have his way in my life. I had asked him to remove the ugly things and any sinful way. I had asked him to cleanse my heart from hate and pain, and I accepted that He would work things out His way, knowing it was for my good. I was the rose bush, untidy and in desperate need of pruning. Every circumstance in my life was a thorn or thistle that had made me harsh and abrasive. I smiled. The pruning process had begun. God was restoring me. He had begun to shape and mold me, removing the hate and the pain.

I knew what I needed to do next. I called my attorney and told him I simply wanted to move on. I explained that I didn't want anything except custody of my children. I didn't want to fight. I didn't want to go to court. I simply wanted to move on. I asked him to settle. "Sell the house, divide property. Sure I'll go to mediation; I simply want to move on." I realized the marriage had been long over, and punishing my husband for his abuse was not my role, my intension or even my wish. I would leave him to the prosecutor. I would tell the truth if called, but I had no desire to destroy him or his career. I didn't want to see any harm come to him, I wanted to see him whole, healed and happy so he could be a father to the boys. But, I didn't want the marriage with him. My goal was to become whole again and make certain that my boys grew up to be productive young men. As I explained the divorce to the boys I prayed with them asking God to protect their father and bring him to a place of reconciliation with God. Every chance I got, I prayed for him, more than I prayed for myself because I knew that his soul was being tormented. My heart and mind were clear of malice and I was ready to start over.

I resolved that if I needed to start over again from ground up, then so be it. I had lost everything, but I was ok. My pastor is known to say: "if you lose everything and you have God, you have enough to start over again". That is where I was. I would start over. I thought of the money he had taken and I smiled knowing that God would return to me everything that was taken. The only thing I would do from then on was simply tell my story with the goal of impacting other women who felt hopeless, lost, invisible, afraid and quieted.

I had also agreed to meet with the prosecutor and to write a victim impact statement because this had truly impacted and changed our lives. I recall listening to the 911 recording in the prosecutor's office. The woman on the call sounded tired. The woman on the phone didn't know who she was. That wasn't me anymore, I had resolved to move forward.

The impact statement was a request from the prosecutor's office regarding the crime of family violence. The purpose of the statement is to determine the impact of the crime on that victim. I copied my journal notes I had written for my therapist detailing incidents that occurred during the marriage. I thought someone needed to know what I went through and I had hoped someone would care. Unfortunately, after almost a year at the district attorney's office, the case was dismissed. There was no deferred adjudication as indicated, there was no meeting with attorneys, and there was no probationary period. His powerful attorney, paid with my money, was able to get him off free from any obligation. My beautiful monster of a husband had no penance for his abuse. The case simply went away, and I with it, as though I never existed. It was hurtful initially, but I knew God had His hand guiding my life, so I accepted the news and let it go making one call to my therapist. She reminded me of the strength and resolve which was exactly what I needed to proceed.

Because I had revisited these painful issues, and although I was healing from shedding the secrets, the act of recalling the events caused me serious trauma and pain and I had to search deep within to overcome that hurdle. It was not something that my therapist could help me with; she had already given me the tools, I simply needed to implement it. I made a conscious decision that every day I awoke I would make a concerted effort to remind myself of who I was in the sight of God. I reminded myself:

I was strong; I was wonderfully and fearfully made; I was the head and not the tail; that I lived in abundance and not in lack, and no matter what weapon came across, it would not prosper against me.

I would make certain to journal throughout the day. I kept my iPad with me, and whenever I had a negative thought I immediately combated it with a positive Scripture. I began reading positive books regularly. Then I turned to the very thing I had detested, church counseling. It was the very thing that I needed.

My therapist had given me the tools to heal. She was critical and instrumental in helping me recognize where I was in my healing process. I began to recall all the Scriptures I learned as a child and as a young adult, and I spoke them out loud combating each negative thought. It was my relationship with God that I needed to reestablish in order to move forward. I had been going through the process of change for almost thirteen years, but I was trying to do it on my own.

After my divorce was final about a year after the last physical altercation, I began to process how my life had changed. I was no longer afraid of hurting anyone, I wasn't afraid of speaking my mind. There is something about speaking positive things; it changes the outlook and the eventual outcome. I changed my mindset as well as the people who were around me as I worked hard to focus on only positive things. If people began to speak doom and gloom or even gossip about others, I shifted. I became deliberate in who I allowed in my space and on whom I spent my emotions. Most importantly, I gained back my worship to God.

Although I had been a worship leader, I didn't feel free. I recall listening to songs about the freedom of worship and the presence of God, but I had a challenging time getting to the presence. I had been filled with so much stuff that I had learned to guard my heart even against the presence of God in worship. When I changed my mindset my environment shifted as my pruning began, and I was immediately transformed. I began each day with worship and praise. I truly felt free to dance without restraint. This was important to me because I had not had the freedom to express myself before.

The Process of Change

How does one forgive? How do I forgive and forget? How do I move past the hurt and devastation? This was a challenging concept for me because I lived in anger and hurt for a very long time. One of the concepts to which I was introduced was the theoretical process of change. Of the several handouts my advocate had given me to review I reflected on the process of change. First of all, I had already been exposed to all of this information as a social worker in the child advocacy world; but, I did not apply it to my life. Therefore, when my advocate gave me the handouts, although they were familiar to me, I needed to still absorb the information. How does one go through change? How did I go through it? It was one of the most difficult periods of my life because first I had to acknowledge and admit where I was in life. Admitting and acknowledging that all my decisions were not well thought out, is tough. I also had to recognize that I needed help to get to the next step and that my way was not working. When I was able to verbalize it I was able to set a plan in action. I also had to confront my past. There are times when the past has to be confronted; the root has to be addressed in order to move past. If the root is sick the tree won't grow. This is same for our mental, emotional and spiritual health. I've heard the saying: trace it and erase it; meaning find the root of the problem and work on it.

Thirdly, preparation is the key to the change process. I prepared my mind with prayer and worship. There is no way I could have made it through without my relationship with God. It was truly my peace. Additionally, I opened myself up to help, by speaking with a therapist and even church counseling. Finally, I set small goals and a vision plan knowing that I had to start over. I recognized where I was currently and envisioned where I wanted to be and created a step by step outline of how I was going to get there.

Here are the Stages of Change

Theoretical change is a process. In the theoretical model, change is a "process involving progress through a series of stages."

Pre-contemplation (Not Ready)-People are not intending to take action in the foreseeable future, and can be unaware that their behavior is problematic
Contemplation (Getting Ready)-People are beginning to recognize that their behavior is problematic, and start to look at the pros and cons of their continued actions
Preparation (Ready)-People are intending to take action in the immediate future, and may begin taking small steps toward behavior change
Action – People have made specific overt modifications in modifying their problem behavior or in acquiring new healthy behaviors
Maintenance – People have been able to sustain action for at least six months and are working to prevent relapse

Termination – Individuals have zero temptation and they are sure they will not return to their old unhealthy habit as a way of coping.

This theoretical outline enabled me to understand, as well as begin, the process of change. Change is never easy, particularly when one has normalized a certain way of living. I was in the maintenance stage when I was introduced to this concept. I believe this was the most challenging phase for me. I had been in the preparatory stage for a number of years, but didn't know how to get over the hump of actually leaving. It took the last act of physical violence, as well as the understanding of the cycle of violence, in order for me to get into the action phase of leaving.

In the maintenance phase, my daily questions were, "How do I do this? How do I forgive? How do I move on? How do I not get stuck in the angry stage?" I didn't have a clue of how to move past it until I heard a sermon by Dr. Joyce Meyer. She referenced a story about an old desk that was very valuable and beautiful. The antique was given as a gift to a young owner. The gift-giver cautioned the owner to polish the desk often and keep it in a cool part of the house away from harsh summer's heat. However, the new owner did not polish the desk as recommended; he did not know the value of the desk and he wasn't careful with its care. It was exposed to harsh weather, the sun as well as the rain from an open window. Eventually, the desk began to lose its luster. Although the value of the desk did not deteriorate, its beauty had faded. The owner of the desk, again not knowing its value, placed it on the side of the road one day until someone saw the desk. The passerby recognized its value and acquired the piece. He polished the desk and fixed the cracks and broken parts that needed to be replaced. After careful maintenance the desk was restored to its beauty. The desk was appraised for almost half a million dollars.

In the sermon Dr. Joyce Meyer likened the desk to many people who have had issues or fragments in their life. Those fragments have caused individuals to lose their luster and value, but then Jesus Christ is the One who redeems and restores us back. After hearing the sermon I began to pray out loud that God change my mind and soften my heart, and that He allow me to be open to forgiving in order for me to move forward with my life. For my healing, I needed to rely on my Christian faith.

People who experience some form of abuse need support. My support, was my faith, it was my lifeline. But sometimes my faith was lacking, I was anxious when things didn't happen as I thought it should. I learned I needed to trust the process like my therapist had encouraged me to do. Then like a ton of bricks this sermon slapped me upside my head. God had forgiven me although I continued to forsake Him, not completely trusting Him because of my own selfish anger. I began to realize that God had removed me from the abusive relationship and restored me. The very things I had prayed for had come to fruition, but I couldn't see it.

I recall I had prayed to God to remove me from the marriage if it was His will. It was not the manner I expected Him to move, but He had moved on my behalf. He reminded me that He provided my every need during the process of divorce, yet I remained angry. Yes, all my money was gone, but every bill was paid every month. I was never in debt regarding my bills. Initially, my friends and family sent money to help me through the first two months; but after the military ordered him to pay me and after I qualified for unemployment, I lived in abundance. Every bill was paid, and I was able to begin saving money. I also tithed to God and every month he increased my holdings. I was in a position to even bless others. God also reminded me that I had custody of my boys, yet I complained. My major concern throughout the process was my children. I wanted them to be safe and I wanted them to live without fear. I knew they loved their father, but I also knew they were fearful of him when he was angry. God inclined his ear to me and gave me primary custody of the children. Then He reminded me that He had birthed a new anointing for ministry in me, but I had not used it

During this challenging season in my life, I wrote everything down. When I began to journal it rekindled my love of writing. I began to write: poetry, plays, and short stories. God continued to give me visions and dreams in the Christian Arts Ministry and before I knew it, I was operating in ministry again. This time, I was not hindered by fear of reprisal or fear of staying out too long. I was able to operate in ministry freely. Everything I did was a fresh start.

I had successfully navigated through the initial phases of the process of change. As my change became more apparent publically, and as I became more established in ministry I needed to forgive. I forgave those whom I felt abandoned me. The first step was to send a message letting them know the boys and I were well and we would love to hear from them. Although it had been over a year of no contact, I swallowed my pride and began to call friends. The questions came like a flood of rain: "Why didn't you tell us?", "Why didn't you leave earlier?", "What made you leave this time?" "Why didn't you trust us enough to tell us what was going on?" and "How can we help you now?" I knew the questions would eventually come, and I was better prepared to answer.

While going through the cycle of violence I was not in a position to confide in anyone. I didn't want the opinion of others to shatter the image I had developed and the façade to which I had grown accustomed. However, as I began to change, as I became more confident in maintaining and accepting the change and growing in who I was, without the marriage, I became more comfortable in telling my friends why I stayed. I found myself educating them on the cycle of violence as well as the process of change. I explained that no one could have made the decision for me to leave except me. No one could have told me how much I could take except me. I explained to my friends that I had felt abandoned by them and they, in turn, expressed they didn't know what to say.

We had become so good at pretending and masking that it was truly a shock to them. Many of their husbands felt they had failed us, particularly me, in not knowing the signs of domestic abuse. The conversations were cathartic to me. With each conversation, my healing continued. I found myself educating my friends on the signs of domestic violence as well as the barriers to a victim's decision to stay. A new passion had been birthed. I wanted to help others who may have been in abusive relationships. I also discovered that some of the friends and acquaintances had somehow had concerns about our relationship or they, too, had been victims during the course of their life. I was being restored and I was beginning to bloom again.

Recalling the story of the antique desk being restored, there had to be a period of shedding, scraping and scrubbing. The sandpaper and scalpel were to cut out and scrub the rough and cracked places to make it smooth. My restoration involved my pride being scrubbed off and in some areas cut off. Like a surgeon the Holy Spirit had to remove some dead areas in my emotional, mental and spiritual disposition in order for healthy new way of thinking to grow. I learned to ask for help. I learned to remove the mask - to be transparent and open. I also learned to take each day as an opportunity to be deliberate and I made certain to enjoy each moment. Every day I awoke, I smiled because I knew that today I would not have to walk on eggshells; no one was going to hit, push, shove or curse at me. I felt freedom for the first time and I loved it.

But God was still working on some areas which still needed pruning. I had a fear of trusting and had closed my heart off. God began to place people in my life who showed me how to depend on others – he gave me ministry partners and very special girlfriends who showed me true alliance. The most significant change which occurred during this time was my conviction. I discovered in order to truly forgive I had to completely change my mind and my thinking. I refused to be a victim and I refused to live in lack. I refused to accept blame or responsibility for his bad actions and I refused to feel guilty about speaking up. I had relearned to let the chips fall where they may.

Coming to that realization took almost nine months. It was the duration of a pregnancy. I had to grow me again, and the rebirth was one of a stronger, more confident me. I knew God was making changes in me, because I didn't fear talking to anyone. I had always been an articulate speaker; but I had an inward fear of inadequacy. Now, I didn't. I didn't apologize for being great, or for standing out. There was no need for my mask. If I didn't like something, I said it. If I didn't care for someone, then I didn't spend time with them. I had begun to bloom in a way that I never had before; unafraid, unabashed and unapologetically, authentically me. Speaking the words of forgiveness released me. It released me from my own demons, from my own prison of fears. In forgiving and releasing him, I could begin to invest in myself.

During this time of rebuilding I met a young minister and his wife who had a dynamic ministry for marriages. I had the opportunity to read a book written by Elder Tyrone Holcomb. In his book, *Marriage Medicine*, the third installation of the *Marriage Matters* series, he states, "God desires for us to live with each other in harmony," and that "it is not God's heart for us to be unkind to each other." He mentions that domestic abuse of any kind is not God's will. I listened keenly to his ministry and purchased every book he had written, because once again, I heard a minister indicate that the abuse was not of God. He didn't blame the victim, nor did he question the act of the spouse, he simply stated that it was wrong.

The validation I had sought for so many years was right there written in black and white. For the first time in thirteen years, a clergyman not only acknowledged domestic abuse in the church, but he also utilized Scripture to support his stance. This was an antithesis to all I had experienced and I felt like flying. "I knew I wasn't crazy," I recall whispering to myself. I made it a point to convey this message to women who lived the same lie that I had. I knew my purpose and I saw the plan that God had for me. I was going to be an advocate for those women who were still silent. I was going to be a voice in the church for those bound by doctrinal teachings.

In my career, armed with sound spiritual direction, I had a new approach with families who experienced domestic abuse but used theocratic reasoning to remain in the relationship with their abuser. I was able to give sound clinical intervention as well as spiritual counsel if requested. I also made it a point not to encourage divorce, because I know couples who have had scandalous acts of betrayal and abuse, yet they were able to stay together and openly move past it to a place of reconciliation and joy. I knew that my marriage was beyond repair because my ex-husband refused to admit he was wrong, refused to admit the hurt he had caused and also refused change. Additionally my heart was hardened against him and I, too, refused to forgive him at that time. But I know intuitively that bad relationships can work if the victim and the perpetrator seek help individually and then collectively. Change is possible if the persons are willing to first admit they are wrong, admit they need help, and then go through the process of change openly and honestly.

My dearest friend and spiritual big brother, John, is one of those people who accepted his role in the demise of his marriage. John ministered to me during my marriage as well as during the process of divorce. He knew my ex-husband and I well, and spoke with us often encouraging us to communicate and give our relationship to God first. He knew a level of our dysfunction, and ministered that God can restore anything if both parties are open and willing. John ministered that he had extramarital affairs while married to his wife of then ten years. One particular affair led him away from the family. He left his wife and two young children and moved into the home of his lover. He knew instantaneously that the relationship was not only doomed, but it would be his undoing. He recalls feeling himself in a whirlpool of dark muddy waters spiritually and could not find his way through. The woman became abusive and one day physically assaulted him with a knife. The person who was at his bedside ministering to him through it was none other than his forgiving and loving wife.

When I asked his wife, my friend and spiritual sister Valerie, why she ministered to him, she indicated that God had forgiven her so she forgave him. It was a process for her, but she forgave him and could easily speak to him about the love and forgiveness of God. John states that he reconciled his life to God, and learned how to love and treat his wife the way God had intended. Then ten years after their divorce the couple remarried each other. They both stated that the road to forgiveness was long, hard and painful, but in time they were able to do so and move on. God had restored because they had reconciled the marriage to Him. Their story has always impacted me. Initially I thought perhaps my story would end with the same result; but intuitively, I knew my ex-husband had hardened his heart and had no desire to admit his shortcoming much less reconcile to God. John and Val have an amazing story that can impact and influence many families; they are a depiction of how to truthfully forgive and move on.

When I made up my mind to let go, forgiving was easier than I thought. There was no agenda, no hard feelings and no anger. It didn't matter if my forgiveness was accepted or not. I could openly pray for my now ex-husband without any reservation. I prayed for him to come to Christ and I prayed that he would truly look at himself and make a change. I prayed that he would be a good father to his sons and I prayed that God would restore him. I knew he felt nothing but contempt for me. He had said in his own words that he hated me. They were the last words we said to each other. I forgave him and he hated me. But we would meet one more time.

A few months after the mediation and finalization of our divorce, I received a call from the military to testify at his military trial. I didn't know what to say, nor was I certain on what I would be asked. I didn't plan on participating in the trial but I agreed to tell the truth when asked.

It was a cool fall morning. I walked into the building and sat by myself in the cold waiting area. Across the room, I was met by stony stares. He sat with his father, his pastor and several other military personnel. They laughed and joked and I heard them say that nothing will happen to him, it was simply protocol. Nobody acknowledged my presence. There were no kind words for me. No one asked if I was ok. No one seemed to care. He was calm and cold. I made certain not to look in his direction and no one offered me any pleasantries. I was invisible. I was alone again, but I felt victorious. It didn't matter what happened that day, I had made my peace and I was resolute with whatever the outcome.

I was called into the room when the meeting started. After almost two hours of testimony I exited the building sweaty and exhausted. I told the truth. And for the first time in our life, I was able to tell him what he did to me and how it impacted me. I had looked directly at him and confronted him on what he had done. I was also able to express to him the impact the abuse had on his children. I wept for the last time mostly because I was exhausted. He sat stone-faced in court, refusing to make eye contact with me. When I was finished and was dismissed, I stood straight up and walked out of the building confident, unshaken and restored. I had taken my voice back. It was time for my new beginning.

Chapter 5

A NEW BEGINNING

I have always been in awe of rain, the peculiarity of its birth and its demise. I thought that rain was mysterious, cleansing, warm and energizing. When I was a young girl I loved standing in the rain, feeling its cool, invigorating life kiss my face. I also loved sitting on the porch watching the rain fall during storms. I enjoyed the enigmatic, large drops as they meandered together to form a pool of water that eventually washed the dirty sidewalk off leaving behind fresh concrete.

Like the concrete porch, I had been washed by the rainstorm of life. The heavy rains had washed the meager existence I had once called my life; I had been drenched and cleansed of my sadness and pain. I was left feeling invigorated. The mourning was over; it was time to live again, it was time to begin again, it was time to dance. After the rain, I have always respected how fresh and clean everything appeared. Life itself seemed to dance and sing after the rain. I, too, was ready to dance. The rain was over, my weeping was over.

I sat in light of the sun watching the rain gently fall against the window pain. My heart smiled. As I observed the course of the rain I once again found myself contemplating my life - the ups and downs, bumps along the way and the new start. Just like the course of the rain drop, my life had taken different turns and twists. I inhaled deeply taking in the smell of fresh cookies. I was home.

The marital property had been sold - a decree ordered by the divorce court judge. My ex-husband had refused to allow the children and I to remain in the property even after the offer was made to buy him out at mediation. Because we could not come to an agreement, the judge ordered the property be sold. We were at an impasse. I recall praying to God, asking Him to have his way in the sale of the home. The property sold quicker than I anticipated. Initially fear gripped my heart. I thought I would be homeless, but then I recalled how God had kept me throughout the almost two-year ordeal of divorce and custody, and within a month I was able to purchase and moved into my own home.

The front room office was my favorite room. The large window welcomed the warm sunrays in the morning and bid the evening sun farewell, filling the office with natural sunlight. I sank into the soft plush couch and tucked my legs beneath me. Sipping my hot cocoa, I smiled as the rain continued to fall softy. The rain fell and the sun shone, both at the same time. *'What a blessing,'* I thought. I looked around the room at the photos I had recently hung on the walls, and I smiled again. My eyes were smiling in the photos and the children were full of life and expectancy. The family in the photo looked hopeful, happy and warm. This was my home. This was my fresh start.

Two months prior, when I accepted an offer for sale on the home, I worried about where I was going to live. I accepted the offer on the marital home on a Thursday afternoon. I went to the realtor on that Friday and signed the paperwork, but I had nowhere to go. I knew I needed to stay in the same city, because I promised my son that he would not have to change high schools. I needed to keep my promise because the boys had seen too much change, too much pain and discord and they desperately needed consistency. But there was nothing in this neighborhood that I could afford on my own. After I signed the paperwork, I drove around the neighborhood before I came home, and there it was. A quaint, one-story, ranch-style home with the "For Sale" sign out front. It was a new subdivision with houses still being built. I parked out front and walked up to the front porch. "This is your home," I heard the Holy Spirit say clear as day.

I peeked through the window. Suddenly I heard someone call out to me, "Ma'am, are you interested in seeing the property?" I thought it was a realtor, but no, it was the builder driving by. I absolutely do not believe in coincidences. I know it was a providential plan for us both to be there at that time, on that day, in order for things to work out the way they did. She hurried to the door chatting happily about the property. I waited for her to unlock the door.

I quietly walked in and immediately I could envision my furnishings in each room. The house appeared to be built and prepared just for me. The builder conveyed that it was a brand new property. The family had backed out because of a major catastrophe in their family. They were unable to close the deal. No one else had shown interest in the house. The house had been on the market for four months. There were three bedrooms and an office space with lots of natural lighting. There was an open floor plan in the living, dining and kitchen area. There were granite countertops and walk-in closets. Although I had a very large home with my husband previously, it was an unhappy home. I knew this modest home, which was considered a downgrade, was exactly the plan God had for me. This was my home.

Once I changed my way of thinking, I began to see things change on my behalf. Although I was frightened about life after the divorce, I knew inherently that I would be ok; I was just unsure of how it would be manifested. I knew that I had to be deliberate in my choices in order not to be dependent on anyone else. But I was unsure of how to go about exerting my new-found independence. I had considered renting, I had considered moving back east to where my parents lived. With everything I considered I thought of my children. I needed to stay. I knew I wanted to purchase a home, but I was afraid of doing it on my own. My prayer was, "Lord please do it if you want me to do it – I mean to have the house." It was a simple prayer.

Trying to contain my excitement, I inquired about the status and price of the house. It was way above what I could afford, more so, I had only been employed for a month. I almost allowed fear to grip my heart, but my pastor, Nathaniel Holcomb, had been speaking on fear. I recalled him saying that when fear grips your heart, that's when faith takes over and faith is action. He also said that I should train my mouth to speak and train my heart to believe those things that God promised me. If God said "He would never leave me nor forsake me," I had to train my mouth to speak those words and train my heart to believe. Although I was still afraid, I began to say to myself, "That house is mine," until I believed it.

Earlier that month, I had received a call from an employment agency that I had never heard of before. The voice on the other side explained that she had a copy of my resume and she inquired if I would be interested in interviewing for the position. Without thinking twice I accepted the offer to interview. The next morning I drove two hours away to interview. It was a mental health hospital and the position was for a mobile clinician. Before I could ask about the position, the Business Director indicated that if I were chosen I could work from home, reporting to the office once a week. I wanted the position! I didn't know how much the salary would be, but I knew I wanted to work from home in this season of life.

The hospital CEO walked into the conference room during my interview and asked me two questions: "When can you start?" and "What do you think your pay should be?" God's favor was surrounding me. I prayed silently and opened my mouth to answer when she quieted me by saying, "Drive home and think about it and give me a call later." I could not believe my ears. By the end of the day, I was employed making a very comfortable salary to care for the boys and myself without any government aid. At that time I had not even dreamed of owning a home, I was simply thinking of selling the marital home. Little did I know, God was working it out for my good!

Now, here was another opportunity, a house. The builder must have seen the concern in my eyes because she said, "That's the asking price, what you can afford?" I didn't know what to say. I was dumbfounded. She encouraged me to speak with my bank and give her a call.

The next week I sat across from the builder to sign my mortgage for a brand new home. The builder lowered the asking price by almost ten thousand dollars and it became my blessing. Within one month, I had a new career and a new home and I was not in debt and continued to live in a surplus.

When I allowed restoration of my mind to take place, I began to shift my thinking from victim to survivor. When I changed my negative energy to positive hope, I began to see people acting on my behalf. I began to see doors opening for me without me lifting a finger. Let me explain. In my new position, I worked from home four out of five days and I was able to be with my children in our new home. Moreover, the builder gave me an incentive deal and waived the mortgage for the first six months with NO interest build up. Now that is favor! I was able to save every portion of my paycheck for the mortgage and rebuild part of the savings that my ex-husband had depleted. God had given me a surplus. I had gone from a frightened victim afraid to leave her 13-year marriage to a strong woman who had the favor of God surrounding her.

The next step of restoration came in the form getting back to me, a better me, a more confident me and a more emotionally and healthy me. How does one begin again after domestic violence? How do you get back to what you lost years ago without knowing exactly what you lost? How do you learn how to trust? How do you apply everything that you have learned in the process of maintaining? Confused? So was I!

I had never really dated so I didn't know how to. I knew conceptually how to pay bills, but I had never had the freedom to spend so I had to learn to establish boundaries immediately. I had never really had real relationships because I was constantly wearing a mask and hiding who I was. The only thing I was certain of was that I was excellent at what I did in my career and in ministry, but I didn't understand personal, open relationships with others. My best friend and I had an open relationship because we had a mutual understanding that had been cultivated because of years of getting to know each other. She knew me throughout the phases of my life, but I didn't know how to be around other women, and furthermore men.

I had always avoided friendships. I kept most women at a superficial level because of the fear of letting them too close to see my hurt, too close to be judged and too close to know the level of my dysfunctional marriage. With men, I kept them at an arm's length because of the fear of being accused of an affair. Now I found myself single. Every fear I had in building a relationship had come to the forefront. I needed to rely on people, I needed to trust people, and I needed the love and support of people. Consequently, I began to cautiously make friends and as a result catch the attention of men. I was absolutely horrified. I didn't want to date. I had no interest in meeting anyone for the purpose of dating. Rather, I had sworn off men for good. I had sworn off ever getting close to anyone. I was beginning to enjoy being single. I enjoyed getting to know my likes and dislikes. I liked the flexibility I had to make my own decisions without consultation to anyone. I liked being selfish. I liked the closet all to myself. I liked not sharing the remote. I liked being alone. I enjoyed just being me. But I knew inherently that God had more for me. I had developed a fear of people, and a fear of rejection. Although I had been strong in my career and in ministry, I had to learn how to love people without the expectation of reciprocation. My fresh start had several layers of learning. I was free of harm and danger physically, but I was in bondage from my own fears of relationship.

My first steps in moving past this hurdle was to admit it, accept it, confess it and address it. My good friend, Presbyter, Dr. D. Edley, began to talk to me about how to be a friend as well as how to open myself to find and to be loved. "In order to gain friends you must show yourself friendly," he had said to me one day. He also said that one day, when I'm ready and after God had restored me I may want to marry again. Inwardly I rolled my eyes thinking "that will never happen." I thought I would start with at least making new friends. This was new territory - scary territory – but, I did it. I met a group of women whom I observed for a short period of time. I recognized that they were honest, drama-free ladies who loved to speak positive and uplifting words to each other and about each other. As I confessed my fear to them, I was not judged. But rather they embraced me, prayed for and with me and accepted me into their circle of friendship. They became my support group as well my social group. It was a small group of three ladies, but they showed me kindness and love. Now, I got it wrong more times than I got it right. I had met many other ladies and groups before I met this group. But I was always made aware that they were not for me; at least not in my current season. As I began to branch out making friends I became exposed to even more opportunities for ministry as well as a career.

I came across a quote from Joel Osteen one day, which read, "You will never rise above the image you have of yourself in your own mind." Like the 10 spies reported, "We are as grasshoppers in our own eyes," I came to the realization that if I didn't see myself as valuable, then I would never be perceived as valuable to anyone. So rather than settling for any friendships, I prayed for the right people to enter my life. Maintaining good, healthy relationships after domestic violence is very challenging. As a survivor, the trust factor had been eradicated. Everyone was a potential threat, so it was critical for me to learn how to trust individuals in my space again.

I was able to maintain working and ministry relationships more easily because there were clear boundaries on which I could focus. However, friendships and personal relationships were not so clear cut. After I was able to establish those few friends that were safe, trustworthy and supportive I continued to grow emotionally and I continued to be restored. Restoration is a process. It cannot happen overnight, or even within a year. Almost four years after the ordeal began and my divorce was finalized, I found myself again at the cusp of yet another change.

I was now comfortable in my own skin. I was content to be alone and content to be with friends. I loved life and most importantly I loved me.

A little over three years after my divorce, I was introduced to a young man - Daryl Frazier - by a mutual friend. I had been on a few dates prior with other friends. But they were not eventful or long-lasting nor were they intended to be. They were more social engagements, re-adjusting to a normal healthy life and by no means serious. But this young man appeared different. He immediately appealed to my cautious mental posture that came naturally. He spoke with confidence, gentleness, wore an attractive personality and most importantly displayed the qualities of a family man of God. One year later we were married and the following year we were blessed with a wonderful son who we named Landon. God had restored every facet of my life. What the devil meant to kill and destroy me, God turned around for my good. The setback of a failed marriage was a set up for a new ministry as well as a new family. I felt like Joseph, from an emotional prison to the palace of mental freedom.

Ministry was growing as well as my career. I had been hired by the local Harker Heights government/Police Department to implement a program working to identify homes which were considered toxic because of domestic abuse, and other social/welfare concerns. My role was to assist these families to obtain resources before a crime of violence occurred. Additionally, I was asked to be an adjunct professor on social issues such as domestic violence as well as child abuse. Furthermore, I was also asked to lecture on identifying and working with domestic abuse at several churches as well as community and church conferences. What the devil designed to destroy me had now propelled me into my destiny. I was being blessed with a position in which my goal - a mission - would be to help women like me; women with whom I now identified, women whom I could now counsel, not only from a place of clinical and evidence-based interventions, but also from an honest place of my own experiences.

Chapter 6

MY PURPOSE
Soaring Higher and Making a Difference

The very thing that kept me in bondage and fear for so many years was now my platform to help restore others. I was now in a position to advocate for those who had been silenced and it was my duty to help them find their voice. I knew that because of divine interventions I had the ability to start over, very much like this song I heard many years ago when I was a young girl. The song often played in my head over the years and I had quietly asked to begin again so many times. The song is called "The Potter" and it states:

One day I saw, a potter and some clay,
he molded it, fashioned it, and caused it to obey,
and soon he had, a vessel he could use,
it held his food it brought him life,
no water he would lose,
but then I heard the vessel slipped and fell,

*it's broken now, I didn't know how to put it back
again,
oh my life, was like, that vessel made of clay,
But Jesus made my vessel over, oh won't you
make this vessel over.*

This song brought my life full circle. Often times I felt that my life circumstances, though beyond my control, were a breaking point for me. I felt like that vessel - broken without a useful purpose. But I was given a second chance at life for a purpose. And I decided the purpose for my pain was to bring others out of the quiet darkness of abuse understanding that it was their choice to make.

Many women who are victims of sexual abuse and/or domestic violence don't get the second chance that I did. Many women who are victims of violence die trying to get away, or they die still in the relationship without knowing that they can live a life free of abuse. National statistics indicate that 1 in 4 women will know domestic violence in their lifetime. Domestic violence and abuse does not discriminate. It happens among heterosexual couples and in same-sex partnerships. It occurs within all age ranges, ethnic backgrounds, and economic levels. And while women are more commonly victimized, men are also abused—especially verbally and emotionally, although sometimes even physically as well. The bottom line is that abusive behavior is never acceptable, whether it's coming from a man, a woman, a teenager, or an older adult. It is critical to let the victims know that they deserve to feel valued, respected, and safe.

One of the most important things that I have learned in talking to individuals about domestic abuse is the need to teach elders, pastors, teachers, women's groups, and other communities to recognize the signs of domestic abuse. It is critical to know that violence often escalates from threats and verbal abuse to violence. And while physical injury may be the most obvious danger, the emotional and psychological consequences of domestic abuse are also severe. Emotionally abusive relationships can destroy your self-worth, lead to anxiety and depression and make you feel helpless and alone. No one should have to endure this kind of pain, and your first step to breaking free is recognizing that your situation is abusive. Once you acknowledge the reality of the abusive situation, then you can get the help you need.

Signs of an abusive relationship

There are many signs of an abusive relationship. The most telling sign is fear of your partner. If you feel like you have to walk on eggshells around your partner—constantly watching what you say and do in order to avoid a blow-up—chances are your relationship is unhealthy and abusive. Other signs that you may be in an abusive relationship include a partner who belittles you or tries to control you, and feelings of self-loathing, helplessness, and desperation. I would strongly encourage you to seek help from a professional should you ever find yourself feeling this way about a relationship. Church elders and pastors are well-intended and they are also a great resource for spiritual help; but, unfortunately most aren't properly trained in the field of abuse. They are able to speak on spiritual issues with a degree of competence, however, in these instances, emotional and mental health counseling is needed. This by all means does not negate Christian counseling.

To determine whether your relationship is abusive, answer the questions below. The more "yes" answers, the more likely it is that you're in an abusive relationship.

SIGNS THAT YOU'RE IN AN ABUSIVE RELATIONSHIP

Your Inner Thoughts and Feelings	Your Partner's Belittling Behavior
Do you:	**Does your partner:**
Feel afraid of your partner much of the time?	Humiliate or yell at you?
Avoid certain topics out of fear of angering your partner?	Criticize you and put you down?
Feel that you can't do anything right for your partner?	Treat you so badly that you're embarrassed for your friends or family to see?
Believe that you deserve to be hurt or mistreated?	Ignore or put down your opinions or accomplishments?
Wonder if you're the one who is crazy?	Blame you for their own abusive behavior?
Feel emotionally numb or helpless?	See you as property or a sex object, rather

SIGNS Continued

Your Partner's Violent Behavior or Threats	Your Partner's Controlling Behavior
Does your partner:	**Does your partner:**
Have a bad and unpredictable temper?	Act excessively jealous and possessive?
Hurt you, or threaten to hurt or kill you?	Control where you go or what you do?
Threaten to take your children away or harm them?	Keep you from seeing your friends or family?
Threaten to commit suicide if you leave?	Limit your access to money, the phone, or the car?
Force you to have sex?	**Deliberately inflicts pain during sex**
Destroy your personal belongings?	Constantly check up on your activity?

Domestic abuse is not simply limited to these acts or concerns. When people talk about domestic violence, they are often referring to the physical abuse of a spouse or intimate partner. Physical abuse is the use of physical force against someone in a way that injures or endangers that person. Physical assault or battering is a crime, whether it occurs inside or outside of the family. The police have the power and authority to protect you from physical attack. Domestic family or spousal abuse is not only the act of physical violence, it is also the emotional, financial and sexual power and control one party has over the other.

The National Center for Domestic Violence asserts that domestic violence occurs when one person in an intimate relationship exercises power and control over the other through a pattern of intentional behaviors, including psychological, emotional, physical, and sexual abuse. There is no way to define a "typical" victim of domestic violence--it can affect anyone from any socioeconomic, demographic, geographic, or educational background. The greatest risk factor for victimization is simply being a woman.

When people think of domestic abuse, they often picture battered women who have been physically assaulted. As you have read from my story, I did not appear as a typical victim may be portrayed. I wasn't covered in bruises on a daily basis. I was proficient in covering up. Know that not all abusive relationships involve physical violence. Just because you're not battered and bruised doesn't mean you're not being abused. Many men and women suffer from emotional abuse, which is no less destructive. Unfortunately, emotional abuse is often minimized or overlooked, even by the person being abused. The aim of emotional abuse is to chip away at your feelings of self-worth and independence. If you're the victim of emotional abuse, you may feel that there is no way out of the relationship or that without your abusive partner you have nothing.

Emotional abuse includes verbal abuse such as yelling, name-calling, blaming and shaming. Isolation, intimidation, and controlling behavior also fall under emotional abuse. Additionally, abusers who use emotional or psychological abuse often throw in threats of physical violence or other repercussions if you don't do what they want.

You may think that physical abuse is far worse than emotional abuse, since physical violence can send you to the hospital and leave you with scars. But, the scars of emotional abuse are very real, and they run deep. In fact, emotional abuse can be just as damaging as physical abuse—sometimes even more so.

Despite what many people believe, domestic violence and abuse is not due to the abuser's loss of control over his or her behavior. In fact, abusive behavior and violence is a deliberate choice made by the abuser in order to control you.

Abusers use a variety of tactics to manipulate you and exert their power:

· **Dominance** – Abusive individuals need to feel in charge of the relationship. They will make decisions for you and the family, tell you what to do, and expect you to obey without question. Your abuser may treat you like a servant, child, or even as his or her possession.

· **Humiliation** – An abuser will do everything he or she can to make you feel bad about yourself or defective in some way. After all, if you believe you're worthless and that no one else will want you, you're less likely to leave. Insults, name-calling, shaming, and public put-downs are all weapons of abuse designed to erode your self-esteem and make you feel powerless.

· **Isolation** – In order to increase your dependence on him or her, an abusive partner will cut you off from the outside world. He or she may keep you from seeing family or friends, or even prevent you from going to work or school. You may have to ask permission to do anything, go anywhere, or see anyone.

· **Threats** – Abusers commonly use threats to keep their partners from leaving or to scare them into dropping charges. Your abuser may threaten to hurt or kill you, your children, other family members, or even pets. He or she may also threaten to commit suicide, file false charges against you, or report you to child services.

· **Intimidation** – Your abuser may use a variety of intimidation tactics designed to scare you into submission. Such tactics include making threatening looks or gestures, smashing things in front of you, destroying property, hurting your pets, or putting weapons on display. The clear message is that if you don't obey, there will be violent consequences.

· **Denial and blame** – Abusers are very good at making excuses for the inexcusable. They will blame their abusive and violent behavior on a bad childhood, a bad day, and even on the victims of their abuse. Your abusive partner may minimize the abuse or deny that it occurred. He or she will commonly shift the responsibility on to you; somehow, his or her violent and abusive behavior is your fault.

It is important to note that domestic violence does not always manifest as physical abuse. Emotional and psychological abuse can often be just as extreme as physical violence. Lack of physical violence does not mean the abuser is any less dangerous to the victim, nor does it mean the victim is any less trapped by the abuse.

Additionally, domestic violence does not always end when the victim escapes the abuser, tries to terminate the relationship, and/or seeks help. Often, it intensifies because the abuser feels a loss of control over the victim. The National Center for Domestic Violence indicated that abusers frequently continue to stalk, harass, threaten, and try to control the victim after the victim escapes. In fact, the victim is often in the most danger directly following the escape from the relationship or when they seek help; 1/5 of homicide victims with restraining orders are murdered within two days of obtaining the order; 1/3 are murdered within the first month. The statistics also go on the say that 2 women die each day at the hand of their abuser. So why does she stay? Why would someone put themselves through such pain? Why doesn't she leave?

One of the most unfair questions asked is: "Why didn't she just leave?" As you read, many times I tried and many times I felt stuck. There are many victims who are undocumented immigrants, or uneducated, or financially dependent on their abuser. There are many victims who are unaware of any other way to live because of generational abuse and dysfunction. And there are victims who just don't

160

see a way out because of lack of support or resources. Whatever the barrier, victims aren't asking to be abused. I assure you that no one goes into a relationship expecting to be abused.

There are many different barriers as to why victims remain with their abuser. Unfair blame is frequently put upon the victim of abuse because of assumptions that victims choose to stay in the abuse. The truth is, bringing an end to abuse is not a matter of the victim choosing to leave; it is a matter of the victim being able to safely escape their abuser, or the abuser choosing to stop the abuse, or criminally holding the abuser accountable for the abuse they inflict. Whatever the case, victims need to feel safe. Victims need to feel supported and victims need to know that they can trust again. The best thing you can do if you suspect someone is being abused is to be that trustworthy support they need. Don't blame, or shame the victim. Help the victim develop a safety plan and listen.

Maintaining after leaving the relationship is the most challenging part. If someone you care about has left an abusive relationship, this is the most challenging time. Keep your word to them. Support by listening attentively without blame. Why they stayed is secondary; praise and support them for the courage it took to leave. This person needs a friend who is not judgmental or critical of their choices, and they need someone who will allow them to finally be themselves.

If you have come to the realization that you are a victim please know there is help for you. Call your local police department and inquire about shelters or resources in your area. Develop a plan to keep yourself and children safe. Talk to someone you trust, and keep talking until someone hears you. You are not alone in this.

I recognize that I was not alone on this journey and am so thankful for the people who helped me to reach this point. I learned a lot during the process of change. I also learned a great deal through the unpleasant experiences with my ex-husband, but most importantly I learned much more about myself through the adversity, which enabled me to get up and move forward toward a new beginning.

In spite of the negative events (abused as a child, raped, and beaten), a resolve was inculcated that allowed me to survive with the help and support of my parents, family members, a few friends and most of all my Lord and Savior. The behaviors leveled at me were meant to destroy and kill – but they did not; neither did they made me bitter, but rather served as the driving force propelling me into a greater destiny for good. Restored, my mourning was turned into dancing. The same can be your testimony today.

If you are in danger call for help!

Call 911 for immediate help!

If you need support or advice call
The National Domestic Violence Hotline.

24/7 Phone Support

Trained advocates are available to take your calls through our toll free, 24/7 hotline at
1-800-799-SAFE FREE (7233).

BIBLIOGRAPHY

James Strong, LL.D., S.T.D. The New Strong's Expanded Exhaustive Concordance of the Bible. Nashville, TN: by Thomas Nelson Publishing

Life Beyond Fear Nate Holcomb (2012) it's All About Him Publishing, INC.

Marriage Matters (Learning to Love Like God) Tyrone Holcomb (2009) It's All About Him Publishing, INC

Online Etymology Dictionary. Retrieved July 11, 2015, from Dictionary.com website: ttp://dictionary.reference.com/browse/parabole

http://www.ncadv.org/need-support/what-is-domestic-violence

Davies, J. Lyons, E. Domestic Violence Advocacy (2nd Edition) Complex Lives/Difficult Choices (2014) Sage Publishing

Jacqueline C. Campbell, PHD., R.N., www.dangerassessment.com

John and Valerie Dyson – Personal Interview

To contact the author for speaking engagements or dramatic presentations please email:

Minister Kerry Ann Frazier at:

KERRYZAMORE@YAHOO.COM

Or visit my website

www.kerry-annfrazier.com

www.ingramcontent.com/pod-product-compliance
Lightning Source LLC
LaVergne TN
LVHW051122080426
835510LV00018B/2186